Marilyn Hickey is a woman of the Word. God is using her to recognize and communicate Bible truth so clearly and forcefully that faith for salvation is born in the hearts of the unsaved, and grace for practical Christian living is bestowed upon believers.

—Joyce Meyer
Founder, Joyce Meyer Ministries
Fenton, Missouri

Marilyn Hickey's ministry is making an unprecedented impact worldwide by spreading the Word of God and His delivering power. She is a mighty woman of God and a great leader for God.

—Oral Roberts
Founder, Oral Roberts Ministries and
Oral Roberts University
Tulsa, Oklahoma

I recommend her ministry highly to all churches, ministries, and people groups. She is a real model of a godly woman in every respect, and her ministries are all outstanding.

—Rev. Dr. David Yonggi Cho
Pastor, Yoido Full Gospel Church
Seoul, South Korea

Marilyn Hickey Ministries has made a major impact on many nations of the world. Her teaching opens the Word of God and sets the captives free. I highly recommend it.

—Cindy Jacobs
Cofounder, Generals International
Dallas, Texas

I believe Marilyn is on the cutting edge of world evangelism. She has the pulse beat of the Third World in her heart. In my last crusade in India, Marilyn spoke to over 200,000 precious Indian people, and I saw the Lord move in a powerful way. I am honored to be her friend and co-laborer in these last days!

—Dick Bernal
Founder/Senior Pastor, Jubilee Christian Center
San Jose, California

TOTAL
Healing

Marilyn HICKEY

WHITAKER
HOUSE

TOTAL HEALING

Revised and updated edition
(Based on the previously published title *Be Healed*)

ISBN: 978-1-60374-267-2
Printed in the United States of America
© 1992, 2011 by Marilyn Hickey Ministries

Marilyn Hickey Ministries
P.O. Box 6598
Englewood, CO 80155
www.marilynandsarah.org

Whitaker House
1030 Hunt Valley Circle
New Kensington, PA 15068
www.whitakerhouse.com

Library of Congress Cataloging-in-Publication Data
Hickey, Marilyn.
Total healing / Marilyn Hickey. — Rev. and updated ed.
  p. cm.
"Based on the previously published title, Be Healed"—T.p. verso. Privately published: Englewood, CO : Marilyn Hickey Ministries, ©1992.
  Summary: "International Bible teacher Marilyn Hickey explains how to be healed and live in divine health through biblical truths and principles and relates compelling accounts of people who have been healed"—Provided by publisher.
  ISBN 978-1-60374-267-2 (trade pbk. : alk. paper) 1. Spiritual healing. 2. Healing—Religious aspects—Christianity. 3. Health—Religious aspects—Christianity. I. Hickey, Marilyn. Be healed. II. Title.
  BT732.5.H53 2011
  234'.131—dc22
                              2011000123

3 4 5 6 7 8 9 10 11 12 **WH** 20 19 18 17 16 15 14 13

Contents

God Wants You Well

I n Jesus' name, *be healed*!" Power, like a million volts of electricity, issued from those words. Instantly, the woman felt God's touch on her body, and she knew she was being healed. She actually felt the large fibroid tumor that had invaded her body begin to shrink; she could even watch her body regain its normal shape.

Only a miracle had kept the woman alive for nearly five years. The tumor had been gradually snuffing out her life. Wrapping itself around the internal organs of her body, it had pushed out her stomach and shoved the lower abdominal organs upward against her heart and lungs. The woman had felt the tumor inching its way toward her heart. Nevertheless, her spiritual "heart" remained fixed in God, and every day she lived, she lived expecting a miracle. "I will not die but live and declare the works of the Lord" she repeatedly reminded herself as she quoted Psalm 118:17.

The woman's condition had been diagnosed and confirmed by several doctors. Although they knew what was happening, none of them dared operate because it was riskier to attempt a removal of the tumor than it was to leave the tumor alone. It was a no-win situation. Gradually, her life was ebbing away. The tumor was bad enough, but the hemorrhaging caused by the tumor was even more threatening. Blood transfusions would have been beneficial, but the doctors were hesitant because of the threat of AIDS. In spite of her condition, the woman had never given up. At the moment of her healing, she was among a group who had gone with me on a short-term missions trip to China.

Healed by the Great Physician

Somewhere high above the Pacific Ocean, as the big jetliner soared through the skies toward home, *the miracle* happened! God had spoken to another woman in the group, saying, *This thing will not kill your friend; I'm going to deliver her now, as you speak the word of healing.* Then, the precious Holy Spirit gave her a glimpse inside the afflicted body of her new friend. With her spiritual eyes, the astonished woman saw something that looked like a tree whose roots were in the woman's uterine area; then, the "tree" branched out, wrapping itself around all the other organs; and then, it was reaching for her heart.

As the one woman prayed for the other, the power of God enveloped them both and surged into the body of the sick woman. She literally felt the tumor shrinking from around her heart, then her lungs and stomach. After her other organs were released from the tentacles of the tumor, the Lord began putting all her organs back in place. In a matter of moments, God had done what no physician had been able to do in years. The woman was healed by the touch of the *Great Physician*. Documented records confirm the woman's dramatic healing. She was well and rejoicing in the Lord.

How thrilling! I get excited every time I see or hear about a miracle of healing. The Lord is continually showing Himself to be the same today as He has ever been. Let me tell you, God is up-to-date. What He is doing in our day is as current as the headlines in this morning's paper. You don't have to read about His mighty works in the Bible to know that He is your Healer. Whoever you are, wherever you are, you can experience His healing touch this very moment! Over and over again, the Lord is proving that He wants to heal you and make you whole.

> *Whoever you are, wherever you are, you can experience God's healing touch.*

There have always been two kinds of people in the world, those who are well and those who are sick—and the sick are doing everything they can to get well. If you are ill, my heart's desire is that the information you receive within the pages of this book may stir your faith and produce your healing. If you are enjoying good health, you can learn how to stay that way. If you picked up this book because you have a friend or loved one who is ill, I'm believing you'll learn to pray for that person with faith and confidence *and see results*. If you are not convinced that God is your Healer, I believe the Word of God will change your thinking. Whatever your reason for reading this book, I hope it will expand your knowledge and change you in a very positive way. Here's to good health!

The Pursuit of Healing

Few topics capture our interest and attention more than health and healing. Much of our time and money is spent on pursuing good health. Medicine has become so specialized that it seems as if we need a different doctor for every problem or body part. Large hospitals and medical centers etch the skyline of every major city, and even the smallest towns boast of a clinic. State-of-the-art equipment is able to probe and image the most remote and inaccessible regions of our bodies. Let's face it, medicine has become a trillion-dollar industry, and the cost of staying well is staggering.

Preventive medicine has also come to the forefront in recent years. After all, don't we prefer to stay well rather than need to be healed? We now have physicians who practice only in the areas of nutrition and prevention, and *holistic medicine* has become a byword. Shopping malls have nutrition stores with shelves stocked with every imaginable vitamin, herb, drink, and so forth, all intended to promote health. People watch their cholesterol and triglyceride levels like a financier would watch the latest Dow Jones average. Many of us are running (or walking) after a healthier body. Fitness programs and exercise machines, not to mention health clubs, are all the rage. Has our all-consuming interest in good health become a "new religion" in our day?

Nothing Is Too Hard for God

Yet, in spite of all this focus on health care, preventive medicine, and fitness, there are still multitudes of people who are ill. I appreciate what medical science is doing to improve our health, and I am thankful for every doctor practicing his or her skills to provide healing for our bodies. However, we know there are things doctors cannot do, and you may be one of those who is stricken with an incurable disease. Let me tell you that nothing is too hard for God. There is just no touch like the touch of Jesus!

The unusual healing of the woman I mentioned earlier reminds me of a woman Jesus healed while He was here on earth. That woman had been hemorrhaging for twelve years and had spent all the money she had on doctors; yet, instead of getting better, she was getting worse. It took a lot of courage for her to approach Jesus, but what she had heard about Jesus' healing power had convinced her that if she could even touch His clothes, she would be healed. Her faith was instantly rewarded, and Jesus commended her by saying, *"Thy faith hath made thee whole; go in peace"* (Luke 8:48 KJV). You see, nothing takes the Lord by surprise; everything He has done in the past, He can do for you today.

Several facts catch my attention in the miraculous healing of this woman. Even in a large crowd,

Jesus had time for one "insignificant" woman who touched Him by faith. Jesus knew that the woman could slip away undetected, and she would go with a whole body. However, Jesus cared so much for the woman that He stopped her and gave her His *word* on the matter: *"Thy faith hath made thee whole; go in peace."* He had the power, and she had the faith. What a combination!

Total Healing

When we talk about healing, we almost always think of physical healing, but God's healing is for the *whole* person. He provides total healing. Under the inspiration of the Holy Spirit, the apostle Paul prayed,

> *Now may the God of peace Himself sanctify you completely; and may your whole spirit, soul, and body be preserved blameless at the coming of our Lord Jesus Christ.*
> (1 Thessalonians 5:23)

God wants *all* of you well. His Word declares that healing is for your entire being: your spirit, your soul, and your body.

Notice with me that Paul put the spirit first. Without spirit wholeness, neither your soul nor your body can truly stay in good health. Spirit wholeness means having the eternal life of God in your spirit by asking Jesus to be your Savior. Spirit "wellness" is maintained by a continual feeding on God's Word. Just as your body needs wholesome food to maintain good health, so your spirit needs the wholesome Word of God to maintain good health. You certainly need a strong, healthy spirit to be an overcomer in life.

The Lord also wants you well in your soul. Your soul is made up of your mind, your emotions, and your will. The will is the course-setter and direction-finder of every individual. Being mentally and emotionally able to make wise choices and right decisions is a very important factor in wholeness. Lives can be ruined through bad choices, can't they? Look what happened to all of us when Adam and Eve ate the forbidden fruit. (See Genesis 3.) Now *that* was a bad choice!

Soul "sickness" is often the result of choosing to hold on to anger or bitterness without forgiving others or oneself. Guilt is a terrible tormentor. It might come through a decision to commit adultery, thereby breaking up a home and bringing overwhelming sorrow and depression; or, it might be an error in judgment that brought about a business failure. Whatever the case, we now have doctors and therapists for the soul-sick. Isn't it wonderful to know that it is the will of God the Father for us to be mentally and emotionally healthy, and that God the Holy Spirit can give us the wisdom to make right and profitable decisions!

In the spring of 2007, a mentally unbalanced student at Virginia Tech in Blacksburg, Virginia, shot and killed thirty-two students and teachers, as well as himself, and wounded twenty-five others. It was the worst killing spree by a single gunman in the history of the United States. I remember once reading a headline with the horrifying news of a man so disturbed that he murdered fifteen people, dismembered their bodies, and then proceeded to eat the body parts! Our modern society is flooded with individuals who aren't mentally or emotionally whole. You and I live in a sin-sick world, and only Jesus can make the difference.

Let me share some "good news" that you won't read in the newspaper. A Christian couple went to prison authorities and obtained permission to meet with a female serial killer. When they shared God's love with her, this hardened criminal gave her life to Christ and was filled with the Holy Spirit. The husband and wife, themselves filled with divine love, legally adopted this convicted murderess. Whatever punishment the woman suffered for her crimes, she knew that *"old things have passed away"* and that *"all things have become new"* in Christ Jesus. (See 2 Corinthians 5:17.) What a miraculous healing!

Wholeness is the will of God for every individual.

Wherever you are and whatever your circumstances, *the Lord wants you whole.* If you have a broken heart, He wants to heal it. If you have a broken pocketbook, He wants to heal it. If you have a sick, infirm, or broken body, the Lord wants to heal it. Wholeness is the will of God for every individual, and certainly nothing is too difficult for the One who created the universe and fashioned your physical body. The Lord is able to heal your circumstances and your relationships just as easily as He can heal your body—if you ask and believe.

> *Now this is the confidence that we have in Him, that if we ask anything according to His will, He hears us. And if we know that He hears us, whatever we ask, we know that we have the petitions that we have asked of Him.* (1 John 5:14–15)

> *Beloved, I pray that you may prosper in all things and be in health, just as your soul prospers.* (3 John 2)

2

Made in the Image of God

When God designed the first man and woman, they were absolutely perfect. The master plan was set in motion by God the Father, who said, *"Let Us make man in Our image"* (Genesis 1:26). Then Jesus—God the Son—executed the plan by scooping up a lump of clay and shaping a man; out of the man, He fashioned a woman. In speaking of Jesus, Colossians 1:16 tells us that *"all things were created through Him and for Him."* In John 1:3, we read that by God's Word, all things were made, *"and without Him nothing was made that was made."* John 1:14 positively identifies the Word as Jesus Christ; but not until the Holy Spirit breathed the life of God into Adam's spirit did Adam become a living being. All three Persons of the Trinity were involved.

So, you see, you have been made in the likeness and image of the Father, the Son, and the Holy Spirit. You and I are just "chips off the old block." When God made you in His image—spirit, soul, and body—He was just as interested in your body as in any other part of your being. He is the same yesterday, today, and forever. (See Hebrews 13:8.) When God made our first human father and mother, He was so pleased with His workmanship that He stood back, looked at them, and said, in effect, "Just what We wanted. This is very good." (See Genesis 1:26–31.)

Ecclesiastes 3:14 states, *"I know that whatever God does, it shall be forever. Nothing can be added to it, and nothing taken from it. God does it, that men should fear before Him."* When God made human beings, He made them very complete, very good, and very wonderful. Even many scientists who are agnostics or atheists agree with this idea expressed by the psalmist David: *"I am fearfully and wonderfully made"* (Psalm 139:14). These people can't even begin to understand the intricacies and the beauty of the body. It is beyond them. Why? Because it is made by God, made to be like Him! I want to show you that your body is a gift from God:

For You formed my inward parts; You covered me in my mother's womb. I will praise You, for I am fearfully and wonderfully made; marvelous are Your works, and that my soul knows very well.…Your eyes saw my substance, being yet unformed. And in Your book they all were written, the days fashioned for me, when as yet there were none of them. How precious also are Your thoughts to me, O God! How great is the sum of them! (Psalm 139:13–14, 16–17)

A Traitor in the Camp

Then, what on earth happened to the human family? If God made us in His image and likeness, when did sin and sickness enter the picture? Since we know that God is good. and everything He created is good, how did Satan and evil come into existence? For the right answers, we must look into the Scriptures. First, we find Satan in heaven. God created him as the archangel Lucifer, in whom apparently was invested the sum of all God's wisdom. This angel was extremely beautiful and gifted in every way. He had great musical ability and probably led all heaven in praises to God. Lucifer was also the *"anointed cherub"* (Ezekiel 28:14) who covered the altar of God and was perhaps the greatest of all God's created beings. But Lucifer turned his eyes on himself instead of on God, and, rather than being grateful, he became resentful. You may read about these things in Isaiah 14:12–15 and Ezekiel 28:12–19.

When Lucifer should have been praising God for giving him his beauty, talent, and position, he became lifted up in pride and set himself up for quite a letdown! At the moment self became the center of attention rather than God, *sin was born*, with all its evil consequences. Lucifer decided he would lift his throne above God's throne, and he enlisted a third of the angels, who rebelled with him. Of course, sin could not exist in the presence of God, so Lucifer and the rebel angels were cast out of God's heaven. God's *"son of the morning"* (Isaiah 14:12), with all his beauty and ability, became darkness, ugliness, and evil. Thus, an intense hatred toward God flamed in the heart of the one who became Satan, *"that serpent of old"* (Revelation 12:9), the devil.

But how did the devil set up shop on earth and get into the sickness business? How did he manage to make God's children sick in the first place? Well, the devil got into the sickness business when human beings got into the sin business. God's first family gave the devil just the opportunity he'd been looking for when those two people succumbed to satanic temptation after the devil came to Eve in the form of a serpent. (See Genesis 3:1–7.) Adam and Eve opened the door to sin, and sin opened the door to all of Satan's work; sickness and sin are Siamese twins. Tell me, was there any sickness or disease in the garden of Eden? No, because there wasn't any death or dying; and sickness is just progressive death.

Adam and Eve opened a veritable Pandora's box when they opened their hearts to sin. They forfeited the earth to Satan, who became the "spoiler" of God's perfect creation. Paradise was lost, and so were life and fellowship with God.

The first human beings retained some aspects of their creation in God's image. However, instead of continuing to have God's nature, they received the devil's nature—a nature filled with sin, sickness, poverty, and death. What sort of nature were Adam and Eve going to pass on to their offspring? Of course, a *sin nature.* Satan had managed to poison the mainstream of humanity with all his evil baggage.

Since Satan is the exact opposite of all God's goodness, his touch brings sickness, disease, and pain. The woman with the flow of blood was touched by the devil before she was touched by the Lord. Notice that when Jesus spoke to the woman, He told her to go in peace. He could have said, "Be at ease," and it would have meant the same thing. God's health and blessing bring peace; they put us at ease. So, what does Satan do? He brings disease. Do you realize that when your body is diseased, you are out of the peace God intends for you?

> *God's health and blessing bring peace; they put us at ease.*

The thief [Satan] *does not come except to steal, and to kill, and to destroy. I* [Jesus] *have come that they may have life, and that they may have it more abundantly.*
(John 10:10)

When Adam and Eve *obeyed* the devil, they *disobeyed* God and relinquished their God-given authority over the earth to a supernatural being who was more powerful than they were *without God.* Do you see what Satan purposed? He had flown in the face of God and won. The Lord had made Adam to be "god" over everything on the earth (see Genesis 1:26–28), but Satan usurped Adam's position, and now all that had belonged to Adam was Satan's. Therefore, every earthly thing fell along with Adam and Eve. It fell into the hands of the deceiver:

Do you not know that to whom you present yourselves slaves to obey, you are that one's slaves whom you obey, whether of sin

> *leading to death, or of obedience leading to righteousness?* (Romans 6:16)

Satan isn't just *your* enemy, he is *God's* enemy. He hates you because he hates God and everything that is like God. When the enemy comes with sickness, it is to harm what God has made in His likeness. The devil wants to destroy everything that God loves and cares for; he wants to spoil God's image on the earth. Satan's way of getting back at God is to come against you. Does Satan hate your body? Of course he does. Without a healthy body, you cannot live in the fullness God desires; and *without* your body, you can no longer live on this earth to rejoice in the Lord and bring glory to His name.

Satan knows that every time he hurts you, he hurts the heart of God, because God loves you so much. Every parent on earth who knows the agony of seeing his or her children sick has some idea of how God, our heavenly parent, must feel when we are diseased. Most parents would willingly take the illnesses of their children upon themselves rather than have their offspring suffer. This is exactly what the Father did for us when Jesus went to the cross and died for the sickness of sin. The substitutionary death of Jesus, who was God in the flesh, redeemed us from sin (see, for example, Galatians 3:13); and in that full redemption was the healing of *your* body!

Jesus Paid the Price for Sin and Sickness

There is no reason for any of us to be confused about who puts sickness on us. Jesus took our sickness and disease upon Himself at Calvary. The Lord paid a price for your wholeness that cannot be measured; Jesus redeemed you from the curse of the law by becoming a curse for you. There is certainly no reason why God would put sickness on His children when He has paid such a price to remove it. Would loving parents put sickness on their children to teach them a lesson or to make them love the parents more? That is utter nonsense! Look at the following:

> *Surely He has borne our griefs (sicknesses, weaknesses, and distresses) and carried our sorrows and pains [of punishment], yet we [ignorantly] considered Him stricken, smitten, and afflicted by God [as if with leprosy]. But He was wounded for our transgressions, He was bruised for our guilt and iniquities; the chastisement [needful to obtain] peace and well-being for us was upon Him, and with the stripes [that wounded] Him we are healed and made whole.*
> (Isaiah 53:4–5 AMP)

> [Jesus] *Himself bore our sins in His own body on the tree, that we, having died to sins, might live for righteousness; by whose stripes you were healed.* (1 Peter 2:24)

There are many people who think God chastens His children by putting sickness on them. But that idea is not biblically sound. Oh yes, all sorts of folks have all sorts of testimonies about how, during a period of illness, God brought them back to Himself or taught them many lessons that needed to be learned.

You may have one of those testimonies, and if you do, I don't doubt that for a moment. God is a "divine opportunist," and He is in the business of turning into good those things that were intended for evil. (See Genesis 50:20; Romans 8:28.) Undoubtedly, many people reach out to the Lord when they are sick and distressed. Yet God doesn't have to *make* you sick to get your attention. Sickness is from the devil:

> *God anointed Jesus of Nazareth with the Holy Spirit and with power, who went about doing good and* **healing all** *who were* **oppressed by the devil**, *for God was with Him.* (Acts 10:38)

> *For this purpose the Son of God was manifested, that He might destroy the works of the devil.* (1 John 3:8)

Jesus was anointed with power to heal those who are oppressed by the devil.

Jesus was anointed with power to heal those who are oppressed by the devil; He was brought into the world to destroy the devil's work. Is sickness the oppression of the devil; is it his work? If it is, then the sick need to be healed! Look with me at another portion of Scripture. Luke 13:10–17 describes a woman who had a *"spirit of infirmity"* (verse 11). For eighteen years, this infirm spirit had caused the woman's body to be bowed so severely that she could not stand straight.

One day, when Jesus was teaching in a synagogue, He saw this crippled woman in the congregation.

The Lord asked the woman to come to Him and, laying His hands on her, said, *"Woman, you are loosed from your infirmity"* (verse 12). Immediately, the woman's body straightened, and she gave glory to God. When the religious hypocrites protested, Jesus said, *"Ought not this woman, being a daughter of Abraham, whom Satan has bound; think of it; for eighteen years, be loosed from this bond on the Sabbath?"* (verse 16). When Jesus said this, *"all His adversaries were put to shame; and all the multitude rejoiced for all the glorious things that were done by Him"* (verse 17).

I am always so delighted when a modern-day miracle of healing brings the Scriptures alive. I want to share just such a remarkable healing, which was told to me by a healing evangelist. In one of his meetings, there was a woman who couldn't be overlooked. She was a pitiful sight! From the waist up, her body was completely bent over to one side. She was contorted into a "U" shape and could neither straighten her body nor look up at anything. When the evangelist prayed for her, those nearby heard loud cracking and popping noises, and, to the amazement of everyone, this woman straightened to an erect position before their eyes and was perfectly healed. Hallelujah! What a miracle.

The Sin Principle

The poor woman I described whom Jesus healed in the synagogue had carried around in her body the marks of Satan's curse until Jesus touched her and made her whole. Jesus said that the curse had come from Satan. It had not come from God! After Adam and Eve sinned, the Lord God came back to the garden in Eden, found those whom He had made so lovingly in His image and likeness, and *explained* what the curse would bring to them, to the earth, and to all the creatures of the earth. Remember that all of the earth fell along with humanity's fall. So, the whole earth was off-kilter; it was all cursed. There was now a "sin principle," a *"law of sin"* (see Romans 7:23, 25), working in humanity and in all its environment. Everything was going to obey that law, without God's intervention:

> *For the earnest expectation of the creation eagerly waits for the revealing of the sons of God. For the creation was subjected to futility, not willingly, but because of Him who subjected it in hope; because the creation itself also will be delivered from the bondage of corruption into the glorious liberty of the children of God. For we know that the whole creation groans and labors with birth pangs together until now.* (Romans 8:19–22)

Both Adam and Eve immediately exposed their sin nature, even though they tried to hide it. Adam blamed God, and he also blamed Eve for his predicament. Eve turned around and blamed the serpent. In the next generation, the inherited sin nature was soon exposed when Cain killed his brother because of pride and jealousy. (See Genesis 4:1–15.) Genesis 3:16–19 generalizes the curse, but Deuteronomy 28:15–68 details the curse that comes from the *"law of sin and death"* (Romans 8:2). Deuteronomy ascribes every manner of sickness to the curse. There is no doubt that sin brings sickness, disease, and everything that is "unwhole." (Contrast 1 Thessalonians 5:23.)

Now I want your full attention. I am *not* saying that you have committed sin every time you get sick. There are people who put guilt trips on those who are ill by implying that their sickness is the result of some specific sin in their lives. Remember that the sin principle that brought sickness and death is at work in the earth. Even some babies are born with disease, deformity, or some physical or mental disability, and those precious children have not had the opportunity to sin. Jesus Himself made it clear that it is not necessarily sin in an individual that causes his or her illness:

> *Now as Jesus passed by, He saw a man who was blind from birth. And His disciples asked Him, saying, "Rabbi, who sinned, this man or his parents, that he was born blind?" Jesus answered, "Neither this man nor his parents sinned...."*   (John 9:1–3)

After telling His followers that it was neither the man nor his parents who had sinned, Jesus declared, *"...but that the works of God should be revealed in him"* (verse 3). The works of Satan had produced blindness, but God's work would bring healing and sight to the man. Jesus said, *"I must work the works of Him who sent Me"* (verse 4), and then He proceeded to demonstrate that work. Bending over, the Lord spit on the ground, rolled a small amount of the wet dirt around in his fingers, and placed some of the "clay" on each of the blind man's eyes. Jesus then commanded the man to go wash off the mud at the pool of Siloam. (See verses 6–7.)

It may have seemed a strange thing to do; but when the man exercised faith in Jesus and obeyed, he was given his sight. Jesus told His disciples—and He is still telling us today—that it wasn't blindness that brought glory to God; it was healing! Nowhere in the Scriptures do we ever see Jesus putting sickness or infirmity on anyone. Neither had God done such a thing so that His Son could demonstrate either His power or the Father's power. Although veiled in human flesh, Jesus was the image and expression of the Father. Jesus told the people that if they had seen Him, they had seen the Father. (See John 14:9.) If God puts sickness on people, then sometime, somewhere, Jesus would have done the same.

> *We are new creations in Christ Jesus, adopted into the family of God, where Satan no longer has a legal right to us.*

Even though God does not put sickness on people, has He left us helpless before the ways of the devil and the curse of the law? Of course not! When we acknowledge our sin nature and confess Jesus as Savior and Lord, we receive a new nature that is the nature of God, the same nature that Adam and Eve had before the fall. Consequently, we are new creations in Christ Jesus, adopted into the family of God, where *Satan no longer has a legal right to us*. Instead, we have the rights and privileges of God's kingdom, which enable us to exercise authority over the devil and all his works.

Therefore, we need to know how sickness invades our bodies, don't we? If we are going to be healed, we must first be convinced that it is God's will to heal. I know a family whose members were committed Christians, but they were sick all the time. The children were so consistently ill that the mother joked about having a regular appointment at the doctor's every week. Then, this woman was invited to one of my first Bible studies and heard the Word of God regarding healing. Soon, she was convinced that healing was part of the salvation package that Jesus purchased for us at Calvary. This lady started praying the Word over her children and rebuking the enemy, and she saw sickness flee every time. Years later, she could say that, except for regular check-ups, none of them had seen a doctor in years. She and her family learned not only how to be healed but also how to walk in divine health.

Before we are born again (see John 3:3–7), Satan can load us with all kinds of his evil "gifts," but when we give our lives to Jesus, we can shut the door on any package the devil wants to deliver. If you don't have the door locked, however, the devil and that sin principle will get in whenever possible. Don't forget that Satan *hates* you because you were created in God's image and likeness. Satan wants to destroy that image. When you are born again, Satan paints a bull's-eye on your back, and he tries to get you with his fiery darts. The more committed you are to

Christ, the more you serve the Lord, the more Satan wants to get you. Sickness is one of the best ways to put you out of commission. So, you don't have to sin for Satan to try to give you sickness.

One time, when I was teaching at a Bible Encounter (a Bible study teaching series sponsored by my ministry), I walked to the pulpit and was suddenly overcome with nausea. I was just minding my own business—and God's—when suddenly I was terribly ill. The devil did not want me to stand before all those people and teach the delivering power of God's Word. With God-given presence of mind, I called on our singer to minister another song and then slipped from the platform to look for some sort of container in which to get rid of the contents of my stomach. I spied a wastebasket just in the nick of time. Some of my staff quickly gathered around me, rebuked the sickness in Jesus' name, and asked the Lord for healing; instantly, I felt God's strength flood my body. Before the singer had finished, I was sitting serenely on the platform ready to teach. Praise the Lord!

Culprits and Solutions

Do you enjoy figuring out the culprits in mystery stories? Well, let's discover some of the mysterious ways in which we leave ourselves open to sickness and ill health.

Sin

Although sin doesn't have to be the reason for an attack, sin will always open the door to sickness.

It doesn't matter what kind of sin it is; a bad attitude is no less sinful than murder. Avoid sin; but if you do sin, quickly repent and be cleansed. Shut the door on the devil! God's Word tells us that *"if we confess our sins, He is faithful and just to forgive us our sins and to cleanse us from all unrighteousness"* (1 John 1:9). Sin brings death, and sickness is death attaching itself to us, but *"if we walk in the light as He is in the light, we have fellowship with one another, and the blood of Jesus Christ His Son cleanses us from all sin"* (verse 7).

Many years ago, I became very angry over a situation. A certain person had pulled some bad business deals on people in our church congregation. Although the matter had been handled, I began to meditate on it; the more I meditated on it, the angrier I became. Shortly after that, I came down with severe flu symptoms: sore throat, fever, and the like. Of course, I rebuked the devil and rebuked the devil—without results. You can imagine how shocked I was when the Lord said, *The devil isn't the problem;* **you are**. The Lord showed me how I had opened the door to sickness by allowing bitterness to lodge in my heart. What the person had done was wrong, but I needed to leave the matter with God. Needless to say, I repented of my sin and slammed the door on the sickness—and received my healing!

Generational Curses

Another way we can be attacked by sickness, disease, and infirmity is through the door of inheritance. If someone in your family tree had a disorder, some of that bad fruit may drop on you. That doesn't seem fair, does it? Yet the enemy will enter through any door he can. However, don't despair; the Holy Spirit can bring repair. We can lay the ax of God's Word to the root of that tree, free ourselves from any "generational curse," and stop it from bearing bad fruit in future generations:

> *Those from among you shall build the old waste places; you shall raise up the foundations of many generations; and you shall be called the Repairer of the Breach, the Restorer of Streets to Dwell In.* (Isaiah 58:12)

My husband, Wally, and I knew a man who had a very bad inheritance. All the males in his family for several generations had heart problems. None of them had lived past his forties. That's a dire circumstance to face, isn't it? The man was married and had sons of his own, and he didn't look forward to an early death. However, this man took hold of the Word of God and came against Satan and that evil inheritance. I'm happy to say that he became "hale and hearty," and the doctors gave him a clean bill of health—all because of Doctor Jesus.

Abuse and Neglect of One's Body

In this busy day in which we live, many of us are committing sins against our bodies without fully realizing what we are doing. We often put ourselves under unnecessary stress, don't get enough sleep, and don't eat properly. How many people go without breakfast, grab fast food for lunch, and eat "prepared" food for dinner? You wouldn't treat your dog that way! But we treat our bodies that way. That is sin! If we belong to Christ, we are part of His body, and the Holy Spirit has made His home in us. Those are reasons enough to care properly for our bodies. We get only one body in this lifetime, and it will wear out and die early if we don't take care of it.

> *Now the body is not for sexual immorality but for the Lord, and the Lord for the body. And God both raised up the Lord and will also raise us up by His power.*
> (1 Corinthians 6:13–14)

> *Or do you not know that your body is the temple of the Holy Spirit who is in you, whom you have from God, and you are not your own? For you were bought at a price; therefore glorify God in your body and in your spirit, which are God's.* (verses 19–20)

When God created the universe, every part was made to function in harmony with every other part, and He set certain laws or principles in motion to keep it that way. Our bodies are no exception, because they are part of God's universal creation. I've found that we don't operate well outside of God's principles. Unless we obey laws of good nutrition and good health, we will become run-down and sick and be susceptible to disease. In the beginning, God prepared an earth system that was compatible with our bodies: fresh air, clean water, and rich soil to bring

Unless we obey laws of good nutrition and good health, we will become run-down and be susceptible to disease.

forth good food. I know mankind today is ruining the environment, but we can do our part to change this and believe the Lord to keep us healthy when we trust Him and obey His Word and His principles: *"But if the Spirit of Him who raised Jesus from the dead dwells in you, He who raised Christ from the dead will also give life to your mortal bodies through His Spirit who dwells in you"* (Romans 8:11).

"I Am Willing"

Let's look at another incident in Jesus' earthly ministry that makes very clear God's will about healing. You may read the account in both Matthew 8 and Mark 1. Our Lord had been teaching and working miracles in the towns around Galilee. Because Jesus' fame had spread through the entire region, a certain man who was diseased with leprosy had heard about the Healer. He did what any man in his condition might do when news of a possible cure came to him. As quickly as possible, the man made his way to Jesus, but this wasn't any easier for him than it had been for the woman with the flow of blood. Everywhere the man went, he had to cry, "Unclean, unclean," because he was a leper.

No one wanted a leper around, but this man had enough faith to go to Jesus in spite of the people. He forged his way right into Jesus' presence, knelt before Him, and pleaded, *"If You are willing, You can make me clean"* (Matthew 8:2; Mark 1:40). Great compassion for this hopelessly diseased man filled the heart of Jesus. Without hesitation, Jesus reached out His hand and touched the man, saying, *"I am willing; be cleansed."* As soon as Jesus spoke those words, the leprosy left the man, and he was cleansed and healed. (See Matthew 8:3; Mark 1:42.)

Most of us think leprosy was a disease of ancient times. But there are regions of the world where people are still afflicted with this dread disease, and leper colonies exist today. I'm here to tell you that Jesus is still healing lepers! Believe it or not, I received a testimony from a man who was gloriously healed of this disease! In today's society, AIDS is as incurable as leprosy was in Jesus' day. However, Jesus makes no distinction between curable and incurable, today or yesterday. I have seen several people healed of AIDS, and their healing has been documented. Glory to the Lord!

The Whole Package: Righteousness, Health, Eternal Life

When you take Jesus as your Savior, you get the whole salvation package. In that package are deliverance, redemption, and *healing.* The Greek word *sozo,* which is often translated as *"save"* in the New Testament, can also mean to "deliver," "redeem," or "heal." Jesus takes your sin and gives you His righteousness. He takes your sickness and gives you health. He takes your spiritual death and gives you eternal life.

Do you think that is a good package? Even though you lost it all in the first Adam, you regained it all in the *"last Adam"* (1 Corinthians 15:45), Jesus Christ. All the weapons that were formed against you cannot prosper (see Isaiah 54:17), because Jesus came and dismantled those weapons. Praise the Lord!

> *Do not be deceived, my beloved brethren. Every good gift and every perfect gift is from above, and comes down from the Father of lights, with whom there is no variation or shadow of turning.* (James 1:16–17)

3

God Wrote the Prescription

My heart overflowed with wonder and amazement when I saw the tiny bundle the nurse was handing me. What a miracle! I pulled back the blanket and looked into the face of the "most beautiful" baby ever born. I cuddled the precious little girl Wally and I had named Sarah. She was truly a gift from God. For thirteen years, we had cried out to the Lord for a child, and now the answer to our prayers was wiggling in my arms. I thought my heart would burst with love—love for her and love for God. The doctors had said I could not bear children, but a man of God had prophesied a child. Wally and I had nothing but a *promise* from God and *faith*. I must confess that I had accepted our adopted son as the fulfillment of that promise, but Wally had continued to believe God for a child of our flesh. And now, here she was.

Nothing is so mysteriously wonderful as new life. How can anyone see a baby and not believe in

God? I've heard it said that a baby is God's promise for the future. I like that! Sarah is now a lovely Christian woman who ministers nationally and internationally, and together we cohost the daily television program *Today with Marilyn and Sarah.* In the years since her birth, I have seen the Lord perform the same miracle for many other couples who have been unable to have children. God has always been a *life giver!* No problem can ever be bigger than He is!

The Foundation for Healing in the Old Testament

Did you know that the first healings mentioned in the Word of God involved barren wombs? God always has wanted to prove to us that if He can give life when life is "impossible," then He can certainly heal *any* life He has created. God laid the foundation for healing in the very beginning of the Bible, back in the old covenant. Healing for our bodies was not a new thought in the mind of God when Jesus came upon the scene.

The Lord Our God Is One God

Christ was the *very expression of the Father's love* clothed in human flesh. One way He expressed that love was by healing those afflicted with sickness and disease. I want to remind you that whatever Jesus is, the Father also is. Jesus Himself declared, *"I and My Father are one"* (John 10:30).

Jesus told His disciples that to know Him was to know the Father, and yet Philip still asked to see the Father. Jesus replied,

*Don't you know me, Philip, even after I have
been among you such a long time? Anyone
who has seen me has seen the Father. How
can you say, "Show us the Father"? Don't
you believe that I am in the Father, and that
the Father is in me? The words I say to you
are not just my own. Rather, it is the Father,
living in me, who is doing his work.*
(John 14:9–10 NIV)

Jesus continued by telling the group that they
should know He and the Father were One by the very
works that He was doing. (See verse 11.) Jesus was
continually healing all manner of sickness and disease. If Jesus is a healer, so is the Father!

Philip is not alone in his confusion about the
"oneness" of the Godhead. Christians are often accused of worshipping three gods because we worship
Jesus and the Holy Spirit as equals with the Father.
Moses, inspired by the Holy Spirit, wrote these profound words: *"Hear, O Israel: The LORD our God, the
LORD is **one!**"* (Deuteronomy 6:4). Does that word *"one"*
mean only one person? The Hebrew word *echad* or
achad translated here as *"one"* means "united," "col-
lect (thoughts)," "to be alike or together." Unity must
involve more than one. For example, two people are
united in one marriage.

I particularly like the Hebrew definition for
echad that refers to a collection of thoughts. What an
interesting and precise revelation of God the Father,
God the Son, and God the Holy Spirit. They think
alike! Consequently, Their purposes are united,
Their words are united, and all Their actions agree.

When thoughts are spoken, they become words. From the beginning, God expressed His thoughts and purposes through the creative power of His words. The gospel of John tells us that God's Word, which is from the beginning, was made manifest in flesh—*Jesus is the Word of God.* (See John 1:1–2, 14.)

Whatever the Father thought, Jesus did. He always carried out the Father's thoughts with His actions, and the Holy Spirit provided the supernatural power. What unity, what oneness!

God Promised a Healing Redeemer

> *Healing for the body is as much a part of salvation as are healing for the spirit and soul.*

It pleases me to know that the triune God has *never* left His people helpless. Back in the garden of Eden, God announced His plan to provide for humanity's healing. Don't ever forget that healing for the body is as much a part of salvation as are healing for the spirit and soul. After Adam and Eve sinned, God told the serpent, *"I will put enmity between you and the woman, and between your seed and her Seed; He shall bruise your head, and you shall bruise His heel"* (Genesis 3:15). Right then, the *miracle* birth of our Savior and Redeemer was promised. We know that the serpent is the devil (see Revelation 12:9) and that the Seed of the woman is Jesus (see Galatians 3:16). Praise the Lord, Jesus was born from a virgin's womb, and at Calvary He crushed Satan's authority over our lives.

The book of Hebrews makes a lengthy comparison of the old and new covenants, saying that in the new covenant we have a *better* hope, a *better* covenant made sure by Jesus Christ, and a *better* covenant established upon *better* promises. (See Hebrews 7:19–8:6.) Nevertheless, we must not forget that the old covenant is the *foundation* for everything we have in the new. Again, the new covenant was not the result of God changing His mind. Quite the contrary, it was the fulfillment of every purpose established in the old covenant. Whatever "fruit" we are eating today comes from God's "tree of life," which has its roots in the old covenant. (See Genesis 2:9.) Let us therefore look into the old covenant and see the provision God's people had for health and healing.

Healing Barren Wombs

How and when did God make good on His promise to be a healer? As I said previously, the first biblical accounts of healing concern people unable to bear children. You know the devil would do what he could to keep human beings from fulfilling God's command to replenish the earth. (See Genesis 1:28.) How frustrated Satan must have been with humanity's ability to reproduce itself, considering how much he hated even one man made in the image of God. Think about something even more problematic for Satan: he had to try to stop the Redeemer of mankind from being born. Of course, there is no way the devil could outsmart the Lord; and every time the devil tried to stop life, God triumphed by proving He is the giver of life.

It's not at all surprising that the first couple we find in the Scriptures who couldn't have children was Abraham and Sarah. It was Abraham who was singled out by God as the one through whom God's Seed would come. Abraham was a man of seventy-five when God first called him, and, to complicate the matter, his wife Sarah had never borne children. Isn't it just like God to come to this pair and tell them that they would have offspring so numerous they couldn't be counted? However, before the Lord manifested His promise of a son to Abraham and Sarah, He exercised Abraham's faith by having him pray for others who were barren.

This miracle happened in the land of Gerar, where Abraham had journeyed with Sarah and all his household. (See Genesis 20.) Abraham instructed Sarah to say she was his sister and not his wife. There were no children tagging along behind Sarah to reveal the truth, so Abraham thought no one would be the wiser. Why would he do such a thing—even though it was true that Sarah was his half sister? I'll tell you why. He did it to save his own skin. Sarah was extraordinarily beautiful, and Abraham feared that any "red-blooded" man of Gerar would want her in his harem—want her badly enough to kill her husband to get her.

Abraham was right about one thing: it wasn't just any man who wanted her; it was the king. As far as Abimelech knew, there was nothing to stop him. Sarah was Abraham's sister, right? Wrong, on two counts! Sarah was Abraham's wife, and the thing Abimelech was about to do was wrong. God revealed the truth to Abimelech in a dream, saying, in effect, "You're a dead man if you touch that man's wife!" Abimelech wasted no time in returning Sarah to Abraham after he received God's ultimatum, but you can be sure that Abraham was called on the carpet for what he had done. His lie had nearly cost the king's life.

As was the custom, Sarah had been in Abimelech's harem for a number of months, going through an elaborate preparation to become the king's wife. During this time, it became obvious that none of the women in the royal household was getting pregnant, not even the maidservants. Even the king's *intent* to consummate a union with Sarah had closed the wombs of the women. The Lord instructed Abimelech to have Abraham pray for the women. And when Abraham prayed, they were *all* healed. God so amazes me! Here was a heathen king and a heathen people, and yet God healed these women so they could conceive. God's love reaches everywhere!

Now, let's go to Genesis 21:

And the LORD visited Sarah as He had said, and the LORD did for Sarah as He had spoken. For Sarah conceived and bore Abraham a son in his old age, at the set time of which God had spoken to him. (verses 1–2)

In my imagination, I hear the cry of an infant, and I see Abraham bending over Sarah, who is cradling a baby in her arms. The expression on the man's face is one of great delight. Although every father should be filled with wonder at the miracle of birth, this man is looking at a *very big* miracle. Abraham was one hundred and Sarah was ninety. What an amazing moment in their lives! It is no wonder that the elderly couple was filled with awe at the product of their faith.

> *And not being weak in faith, he* [Abraham] *did not consider his own body, already dead (since he was about a hundred years old), and the deadness of Sarah's womb. He did not waver at the promise of God through unbelief, but was strengthened in faith, giving glory to God.* (Romans 4:19–20)

At God's command, Abraham and Sarah named their son *Isaac*, which means "laughter." I believe God was reminding Abraham and Sarah that He always has the last laugh. Previously, God had said to Abraham,

> *And I will make My covenant between Me and you, and will multiply you exceedingly....I will make you exceedingly fruitful; and I will make nations of you, and kings shall come from you....Sarah your wife shall bear you a son, and you shall call his name Isaac* [laughter]; *I will establish My covenant with him for an everlasting covenant, and with his descendants after him.* (Genesis 17:2, 6, 19)

Do you know how Abraham had responded to this miraculous promise? He had laughed at the possibility of having even one son. Soon, God had repeated the promise, and Sarah, who had eaves-dropped on the conversation, had taken her turn at laughing over such an incredulous possibility. But is God a healer of bodies? Yes! Is anything too hard for Him? No! The Lord had favor on Sarah, as He had promised, and Sarah conceived. In due time, she bore Abraham a son in his old age, and Abraham named his son "Laughter."

> *Is anything too hard for the LORD? At the appointed time I will return to you, according to the time of life, and Sarah shall have a son.* (Genesis 18:14)

Barrenness followed in the next two generations like a generational curse. However, God took the opportunity to prove that He, and only He, could bring to pass the promises given to Abraham for a nation and a Savior. After Isaac married Rebekah, they soon discovered that she was as barren as her mother-in-law had been. No doubt Isaac was aware of his own miraculous birth when he prayed for Rebekah. They received a double miracle: twins named Jacob and Esau. (See Genesis 25:21–26.) Jacob, too, married a barren woman named Rachel, who *demanded* that he give her children. Jacob reminded his insistent wife that he wasn't God, but she did eventually conceive. The Bible says, *"Then God remembered Rachel, and God listened to her and opened her womb. And she conceived and bore a son, and said, 'God has taken away my reproach.' So she called his name Joseph"* (Genesis 30:22–24). Jacob and Rachel's other son was Benjamin. (See Genesis 30:1–2, 22–24;

> **If God can give life, He can heal life.**

35:16–18.) Over and over, God proved Himself to be the Healer and Life Giver. In all these examples, I want you to see that if God can *give* life, He can *heal* life. Surely, He can repair and maintain what He has made!

I'm impressed by the fact that God consistently answers husbands' prayers for their wives. The Lord has given a special anointing for healing to husbands because a husband is the God-ordained head of his home. God expects healing to flow through families when husbands and fathers pray for their households. Here, in the very first book of the Bible, we have this precedent given to us. I would say to husbands who are not in the habit of praying over their family members, "Don't be afraid to pray for your wives; don't be afraid to pray for your children. You'll be amazed at what God will do through you."

I know of a wife who didn't want her husband's prayer when she needed healing. Although the lady would ask others to pray for her physical needs, she hesitated to ask her husband because she didn't think he would pray effectively. One day, when this lady was ill, the Lord told her to have her husband pray for her. The Lord said He wasn't interested in how effective she thought her husband's prayers were; if she would ask her husband for prayer, then the Lord would heal her every time. It took some courage and swallowing of pride, but the lady obeyed and received her healing. Her husband always has the opportunity to pray for her now. Listen to me: mighty power is released when a husband prays.

A Covenant of Healing

Some five hundred years after Abraham bounced Isaac on his knee, the nation of people that God had promised had become a reality. However, something had gone wrong. Instead of a mighty people serving God, they were a nation of slaves serving the pharaoh, or king, of Egypt.

What had happened? During a terrible famine, when Abraham's offspring had numbered fewer than one hundred people, they had moved to Egypt. Abraham's great-grandson Joseph, who had become Pharaoh's "right-hand man," had invited the family to live there. After Joseph and the rest of his generation died, he and his accomplishments were soon forgotten by Egypt's leaders, and over a million Hebrews were enslaved by the Egyptians. (See Exodus 1:8–12.)

When Abraham's descendants remembered they were children of promise, they began to cry to almighty God, and the Lord sent Moses to be Israel's deliverer. Moses was used by God to bring plagues on Egypt until Pharaoh was finally persuaded to let God's people go. The climax came when the death angel passed through Egypt, killing all the Egyptian firstborn of man and beast. However, when the angel saw blood sprinkled on the doorposts of the Israelites' homes, he passed over and spared all their firstborn. You see, at God's instruction, Moses had told the people to kill a lamb for every household, sprinkle its blood on their doorposts, then roast and eat the lamb. That very night, Pharaoh told those Hebrew slaves to *get out!* (See Exodus 2:1–12:33.)

God had entered a blood covenant with His people that protected and healed them. A miracle took place the night nearly two million people sprinkled the blood and ate the lamb. Those folks had lamb outside and lamb inside, and I believe those lambs healed every sick person and strengthened every feeble one. (See Psalm 105:37 KJV.) What a beautiful picture of Jesus, our Lamb, who heals and delivers us. The Israelite slaves had been ill-fed and ill-treated, so I would guess that many of them weren't in the best shape. Just think, if only 10 percent of that enormous crowd needed some sort of healing in their bodies, then two hundred thousand people were healed at one time. Is God able to heal a multitude? Well, I guess!

Once, in Hungary, I had the opportunity to see God heal a mass of people. The pastor and congregation of the church where I was teaching were very bold in God and aggressive in faith. For the last night of the meeting, this group secured a large stadium that seated ten thousand people, and it was filled. That evening, I prayed for the sick, specifically those with growths, tumors, or warts. I asked all who knew they had been healed to come to the platform. When one hundred fifty people responded, I was overwhelmed. I had expected maybe ten people to come. That night, God showed me I needed to enlarge my expectations. When large groups of people come together in agreement to praise and worship the Lord, there is a rich anointing to heal the masses. No situation is too big for the Lord.

There was no situation too big for God where Israel was concerned, either. The trials weren't over for God's people when they left Egypt, but neither were the miracles. When they reached the Red Sea, Moses parted the waters and led the Israelites across a dry sea floor just ahead of the pursuing Egyptians—who drowned when the waters closed back over them. God's people should have seen that the Lord was bigger than any problem. Nevertheless, in just a few days, the Israelites were murmuring and complaining because they had no water. That is, they had no water except for the bitter waters of Marah, which they were unable to drink. I think the waters were bitter because the people were bitter.

Here were nearly two million people in a desert with no water fit to drink, but whom did they have with them? Yes, they had the Lord! He instructed Moses to cut down a tree and throw it in the waters; then, the waters were "healed." (See Exodus 15:23–25.) People speculate about what kind of tree would have neutralized the bitter waters, but I know it was a *miracle* tree. Just as the Passover lamb typified Jesus, so the tree typified the cross of Calvary. Because of *that tree*, the bitter waters of sin have been neutralized, and we can drink freely of the waters of salvation. God can heal our bodies, and He can also heal our circumstances.

"I Am Your Health!"

It was here at Marah that the Lord gave to Israel, and to us as children of faith, one of the greatest promises of healing found in the Scriptures. When God made the waters of Marah sweet, He said to the people,

If you diligently heed the voice of the Lord your God and do what is right in His sight,

> *give ear to His commandments and keep all*
> *His statutes, I will put none of the diseases*
> *on you which I have brought on the Egyp-*
> *tians. For I am the LORD* **who heals you.**
> (Exodus 15:26)

Literally, He said, "I am your *health!*" From the moment the Israelites entered into a covenant of healing, they walked in health. For forty years, their shoes didn't wear out, their feet didn't swell, and they were not sick! (See Deuteronomy 8:4; Nehemiah 9:21.) The only times they suffered from disease or death were when they disobeyed God, as we will see.

Do you know that God can keep you healthy? Health is far better than healing! Don't plan on getting the flu; don't plan on being sick. I have an evangelist friend who used to say, "Every winter I get the flu." Sure enough, every winter, she had a terrible case of the flu. The lady didn't realize she was scheduling the flu with her own mouth. When she learned that the Lord was her health and understood how her words were defeating her, she changed her "plans" and her words. No more flu! God warns that we are either justified or condemned by the words we speak. (See Matthew 12:35–37.)

Somehow, folks tend to overlook their minds when thinking of health or healing. People just expect to suffer memory loss as they get older, but the Word says that *"we have the mind of Christ"* (1 Corinthians 2:16)! I'm amazed by a Christian writer whose later years were his most productive. When he was seventy years old, the Lord told him the next ten years were going to be his best. He kept his same ministry schedule, traveled the world, and never took a vacation except to write. When he was eighty, this man asked the Lord for another ten years, and at eighty-eight, he wrote the best book I have ever read, besides the Bible. This man *never made plans to be sick*, and he was healthy until the day he died at ninety. He practiced the three *G*s: God's grace, grit (exercise), and grain (proper eating).

Do people have to get sick to die? I don't think so! I believe that we can simply turn loose and "go home" when we are satisfied with length of days. (See Psalm 91:16.) Plan on having good health throughout your entire life. The blood of Jesus doesn't lose its power or wear out as we get older. However, we must take care of our bodies, just as the man I previously mentioned did. Don't forget, Moses was eighty when God called him; and Deuteronomy 34:7 tells us that when he died at one hundred and twenty, his eyes were not dim, and his natural forces were not abated.

> *Plan on having good health throughout your entire life. The blood of Jesus doesn't lose its power or wear out as we get older.*

During Moses' forty years in the wilderness with the Israelites, he had to endure their exasperating ways. Not far from Marah, the people began to murmur and grumble *again*. Now they were dissatisfied with God's choice of "heavenly" food, which they called *manna*, or "What is it?" In their complaint, they even wished to be back in Egypt, where they could eat cucumbers, onions, and garlic. Those Israelites had a very short memory, didn't they? Egypt meant slavery. Because of their complaining, fire came down and destroyed many of them before they admitted their sin. Moses prayed for the Israelites, and God stopped the fire. (See Numbers 11:1–2.) Yes, God healed their circumstance.

However, it wasn't long before the Israelites were complaining again! They really weren't any different from many people today. This time, these bitter people opened the door to poisonous serpents that bit them, and many died. Life was becoming a classroom for slow learners. Moses prayed for the people once more. The Lord told him to make a brass serpent, put it on a pole, and lift it up so that all those who were bitten could see it and be healed. It seems like a strange way to effect healing, but it worked.

As Moses lifted up the serpent in the wilderness, even so must the Son of Man be lifted up, that whoever believes in Him should not perish but have eternal life. (John 3:14–15)

Even Moses' own sister and brother found something about which to murmur and complain. Have you ever noticed that complainers like to spread around their poison? These two were upset because Moses had married an Ethiopian woman. They had another complaint, also. Aaron and Miriam decided Moses wasn't the only one who should be giving orders. They claimed they could hear from God, too, and that they had the right to share some of the leadership. As a result of their sin, Miriam became leprous. Smitten with guilt and remorse, Aaron begged

Moses to pray for their sister. As a result of Moses' prayer, Miriam was healed. (See Numbers 12.)

Occasionally, I telephone a certain friend living in another city. This person believes in divine health and healing; she has read "every" book on healing and has a library of healing tapes. However, every time we talk, she has some sort of complaint. When I ask how she is, she proceeds to tell me in detail about her latest illness. "Nothing seems to be working out right for me," she will say. And nothing does. I want you to know that if you don't mix faith with God's Word and keep your words in line with His Word, nothing will turn out right for you, either!

It wasn't the desert that created a wilderness experience for the Israelites; it was their complaining. They weren't very spiritual, and *yet God healed them.* Have you noticed that unspiritual people get healed? Even the unsaved can get healed. In the late evangelist Kathryn Kuhlman's meetings, the unsaved received some of the most dramatic healings. I've found that God will heal wherever faith is exercised. God is so smart! Many, many times, healing brings a sinner to Christ. It doesn't have to be the other way around. Often, Christians expect healing on the basis of merit instead of faith. They say things like, "I'm always in church," or "I teach Sunday school," or "I sing in the choir"; but God doesn't heal people who have "earned it."

Ways and Means of Healing

In the case of the Israelites, their sicknesses or deaths were the result of sin. Nevertheless, God healed or delivered the people when they repented of complaining. It amuses me when sickness is referred to as a "complaint." That may be more truth than fiction. However, we know not all sickness is the result of sin. Sarah wasn't barren because of sin, and the Scriptures don't say sin brought barrenness to Rebekah or Rachel. If you are sensitive to the voice of the Holy Spirit, He will tell you when the cause of sickness is sin. Repent quickly and mend your ways, and He will mend your body.

There are times when circumstances press us in to healing. Those barren women were so desperate for children that they pressed in to faith and received their healings. It's natural for women to want children, and in Bible times, it was a shame for a woman to be childless. Hannah was another childless woman who pressed in to her answer. She promised the Lord that if He would give her a son, she would dedicate him to God. When Eli the priest agreed with Hannah's faith, she bore not one child but six children. Hannah was faithful to her promise to God, and that first son, Samuel, was consecrated to the Lord as a small child and became one of Israel's greatest prophets. (See 1 Samuel 1.)

Here is a contemporary example of being pressed in to healing. Death stared the wife of a noted pastor in the face, but she *pressed through* to life. Doctors found cancer in the woman's liver and gave her no more than three months to live. Nevertheless, she said, "According to the Word, I will live and not die!" (See Psalm 118:17.) She chose to look at God's answer rather than at the symptoms or the medical report. Day after day, this persistent lady spoke healing promises to her body and listened to tapes on healing. She *determined* to live and declare the works of God. It didn't happen overnight, but gradually healing came; the doctors could find no sign of cancer. Severe illness pressed this woman in to healing, and her testimony has encouraged many others to press in to God for their own healings.

Let's look at some other marvelous healings in the Old Testament. I'm reminded of the Shunammite woman in 2 Kings 4:8–37 who was also barren. She and her husband befriended the prophet Elisha, who repaid the lady by praying for her to have a son. The little boy came in due time, but, years later, as a young man, he died of apparent sunstroke. Mindful of his miraculous birth, the undaunted woman saddled her donkey and went to Elisha without telling anyone of her son's death. Instead, she confessed that all was well. Elisha responded to her plea for help, went to where the woman had laid her son, and prayed for his life to return. This woman, too, pressed in to healing, and death was defeated.

Although the Shunammite woman exercised remarkable faith for the life of her dead son, I don't believe she had any faith for his birth. It was the faith of Elisha that brought about that miracle. God honors the faith of others when they pray for the sick. *You* can stand in the gap and use *your* faith for a sick person who doesn't have the necessary

You can stand in the gap and use your faith for a sick person who doesn't have the necessary faith.

faith. We have prayed for people who were so ill that they could not exercise faith for themselves, and we have seen them healed. Ezekiel 22:30 tells us that God searches for anyone who will fill the gap with faith so He can fulfill His will to restore rather than destroy. My Bible says that believers *"will lay hands on the sick, and they will recover"* (Mark 16:18)! How about yours?

One of the most unusual healings in the Old Testament is that of Naaman, the Syrian captain. Second Kings 5 describes Naaman as *"a mighty man of valor,* **but a leper***"* (verse 1). Through his Israelite slave girl, Naaman learned of the prophet Elisha, who could heal his leprous body.

The captain lost no time in getting to Israel and the prophet Elisha, who sent word to Naaman to dip in the Jordan River seven times. After struggling with his pride, Naaman obeyed and was healed on the seventh dip. This Syrian had been a cruel enemy of Israel; he had been an idolater. Yet God desires to bring any individual to repentance through His marvelous goodness. Because of his healing, Naaman repented and accepted the God of Israel.

Through the compassion of one little slave, Naaman was no longer a leper, and neither was he an idolater. Naaman went home with healing on the inside, as well as healing on the outside. What a life-changing experience! Can you imagine the joy of Naaman's little maid when she saw her master again? Her compassion for this man touches my heart. She had probably been captured and taken from her home to be this man's slave, and yet she cared for him.

A number of times in the New Testament, we read that Jesus looked upon the people with compassion before He healed them or provided for them in other ways. (See, for example, Matthew 14:14.) Compassion mixed with faith is a powerful combination.

On another occasion, the Lord used Elisha in a most unusual way. Every time the Syrians planned a campaign against Israel, someone tipped off the king of Israel, and the plot was foiled. The Syrian king was furious because he supposed there was a traitor in their midst. However, one of his servants said that the "informer" was Elisha, who was able to know the king's thoughts even when he was in his bedroom. The way in which the Syrian king reacted to this information always amuses me. He sent a large army after the prophet.

How the king thought his men would take Elisha by surprise, I don't know. They didn't, of course, but Elisha made no effort to escape. The prophet prayed that God would put blindness on the men, and then he led the army to Israel's King Jehoram. Instead of killing the enemy, Elisha told Jehoram to feed the men and send them home after Elisha prayed for their sight to be restored. Isn't that a unique healing? First, Elisha prayed blindness on the enemy, and then he asked God to remove it. (See 2 Kings 6:8–23.)

Another healing in the Old Testament is probably the most unusual of all. It also concerns Elisha, or rather Elisha's bones. The prophet had died and "gone to his reward," but his bones still lay in his tomb. During a battle with the Moabites, some

Israelite soldiers threw the dead body of a comrade into Elisha's grave. What happened next must have given the soldiers quite a fright. When the dead man's body touched Elisha's bones, the man was instantly brought back to life. So, even the bones of the prophet were tremendously anointed by God! (See 2 Kings 13:20–21.)

You've heard of good King Hezekiah, haven't you? (See 2 Chronicles 31:20.) Well, the circumstances surrounding this man's healing were truly miraculous. After Isaiah the prophet came and told him to set his house in order because he was going to die, Hezekiah turned his face to the wall and beseeched the Lord for healing. Then, God stopped the departing prophet in his tracks with the latest news bulletin from heaven: in three days, Hezekiah would be healed and live another fifteen years! For proof, Hezekiah asked the Lord to cause the sundial to move backward ten degrees, and God did just that! (See, for example, 2 Kings 20:1–11.)

Some biblical commentators believe that Hezekiah was so filled with praise to the Lord that he wrote ten psalms and added to those ten another four by King David and one by King Solomon, a psalm for every additional year of life. Psalms 120–134 are called "psalms of degrees" or "psalms of ascent." If Hezekiah did write and compile these psalms, then he didn't think of the clock running down, but he saw that every year was another step closer to God. He was on an ascent to God, not a descent to death. Don't you like that kind of attitude? Just like Hezekiah, you can turn your face to the wall and cry out to God for a miracle. Then you, too, will have a song in your heart of praise to God, who is daily drawing you closer to Himself.

Then, there is "poor" Job. He was desperately ill, but he was healed after the Lord showed him that he was self-righteous. Job confessed this sin, took his eyes off himself, and prayed for his accusing friends. With such friends, Job didn't need enemies! Nevertheless, with God's viewpoint, Job saw things from a different perspective, and he lived another one hundred forty years. (See Job 40:1–42:17.)

Many times, God heals people when they get free from wrong attitudes. Bad attitudes are very dangerous. I know of a woman who chose to die with a heart condition rather than forgive her mother. At the same time, several people around this woman were loosed from sickness by releasing their bad attitudes.

> *Many times, God heals people when they get free from wrong attitudes.*

God even healed a cruel pagan king when he changed his attitude. King Nebuchadnezzar was responsible for taking the Jews captive into Babylon, and yet God healed him of a mental breakdown when he admitted an attitude of pride. Daniel had warned the king that his pride would be his undoing, but he didn't listen. One day, in the midst of his boasting, he suddenly thought he was an animal, and God put him out to pasture for seven years. When he finally looked up from the grass and lifted his eyes to God, his mind was completely restored. (See Daniel 4.) I want to tell you that God is still healing minds today, and He can heal your mind or the mind of someone for whom you pray.

A lovely woman on my staff was wonderfully healed of mental illness. From early childhood, the lady had been in foster homes, and it was in the first foster home that she accepted Christ. However, she was not given the opportunity to grow in her new-found faith, and a great deal of trauma and abuse in other foster homes nearly obliterated her consciousness of Christ. In her teens, the woman joined a pseudo-Christian cult that further obscured the truth of Christ. By her late twenties, she was battling mental illness and was often hospitalized for both physical and emotional problems. Prompted by the Holy Spirit, the woman began reading her Bible, listening to Christian radio, and watching Christian TV. One morning, she awoke and realized that the veil over her mind had been lifted and that she was completely healed. She became a stable, happy person, rejoicing in Jesus her Healer.

What about backsliders? Will God heal them? If He doesn't, then He shouldn't have healed King Jeroboam! Jeroboam was God's choice for the ten tribes of Israel at the time when the kingdom was divided into the northern kingdom of Israel and the southern kingdom of Judah. This king got off to a good start but took a turn for the worse. He introduced idolatry to the nation by setting up altars to golden calves in Bethel and in Dan, which the people were supposed to worship. Why did he do this? Jeroboam feared losing his kingdom if the men of

Israel went to Judah to worship God at the temple in Jerusalem.

An unnamed prophet came to Bethel and prophesied against the golden calf that Jeroboam had erected. The furious king reached out his hand to strike the prophet, and, instantly, his hand dried up! The idolatrous altar also broke apart. Can you believe that Jeroboam asked this prophet to pray for his healing? I'm amazed that the prophet prayed and even more amazed that God healed this reprobate king. (See 1 Kings 12:26–13:6.) Nevertheless, the goodness of God leads sinners to repentance. (See Romans 2:4.) God loves backsliders, too, and He wants to heal them and draw them back to Himself.

The Lord used various means and different ways to heal in all of the biblical accounts I mentioned: We saw that prayer healed people. Activating faith was a vital part of healing. The Lord took compassion on people, and they received healing. Others pressed in to healing when circumstances put them under pressure. We also saw unique ways of healing, such as Naaman dipping seven times in the Jordan. Even Elisha's bones gave life to a dead soldier. When the waters at Marah were healed, Moses had received a "word of knowledge" (see 1 Corinthians 12:8) from the Lord telling him to cut down the tree and place it in the waters. What is God demonstrating to us? Simply, that He loves us all. He will use any means possible to bring healing to our bodies because He loves us so much! I believe all things are possible to Him, don't you?

When I am ministering in meetings, God almost always gives me a word of knowledge about someone there. One time, the Lord told me there was someone in our service who had suffered from severe headaches for several years, but He was going to heal this individual that evening. A young man responded when I told the people what the Lord had spoken to me. A terrible motorcycle accident had fractured the man's skull in several places, and, while these bones had been knitting back together, large calcium deposits had formed, causing constant, excruciating headaches. The congregation and I prayed for the young man, and he was instantly released from the headaches. A week later, he testified that he hadn't had a sign of a headache since. Praise the Lord!

At one time, King David was so ill that people stayed away from him because he smelled so bad. Yes, illness can actually have a very offensive odor. David may have had his healing from this terrible illness in mind when he wrote,

> Bless the LORD, O my soul, and forget not all His benefits: who forgives all your iniquities, **who heals all your diseases**, who redeems your life from destruction,...so that your youth is renewed like the eagle's.
> (Psalm 103:2–5)

God will also heal others when we send His healing Word to them. Psalm 107:20 says, *"He sent His word and healed them, and delivered them from their destructions."* What a good "package" to receive, and it's even faster than the U.S. Mail!

As we look at the Old Testament, we see such wonderful healings. Over and over again, God provided healing for His people. I'm so thankful that the Holy Spirit has recorded these incidents and given us promises that are as good today as on the day they were given. God's ways and His Word are the same, and neither ever changes. Before Christ Jesus came, every promise was made sure by the blood of a sacrifice; but now, every promise has been made sure by the blood of Jesus Christ. No wonder the book of Hebrews says that we have *"better promises"* (Hebrews 8:6). Aren't you thankful that you can change the circumstance of physical illness with the unchanging Word of God? The Lord is just as concerned for you today as He has ever been for anyone.

You can change the circumstance of physical illness with the unchanging Word of God.

4

Calling Doctor Jesus

The doctor shook his head in utter amazement. What he found in his examination just couldn't be. There was no way the stem of the woman's eye could have reconnected to the eyeball. Every manner of treatment, even surgery, had proven useless, and blindness had been inevitable for his patient. Nevertheless, the woman sitting in the examination chair confirmed his findings; her vision in both eyes was perfectly clear.

With no hope of recovery except for a miracle, this woman had attended a healing service, and what doctors and medical science had not been able to do, the Lord had done in an instant. Not only did the woman's doctor confirm in writing this remarkable healing, but she also has written confirmation from another doctor. God had taken the "im" out of impossible again! This is the kind of thing Jesus does all the time.

Jesus' love for us knows no boundaries, and neither does His healing power.

Since Jesus paid the price for our healing, it just makes sense to me that He would continually prove it in bodies all over the world. His love for us knows no boundaries, and neither does His healing power. Although God is unlimited, Jesus suffered, for your sake and mine, the limitations of a human body in order to pay the awful price for our physical healing. Isaiah foretold it, and Jesus confirmed it: *"by His stripes we are healed"* (Isaiah 53:5)!

Healing Was in the Atonement

Let's look again at the prophecy given by the Lord to Isaiah concerning the healing work of the Messiah. In chapter 53, the prophet began by wondering who had believed his report, but he declared that the work is sure, whether it is believable or not. To this day, many do not believe in the healing work of Calvary, but that makes it no less certain. There are multitudes of people who can *verify* that Jesus is a healer. The woman I mentioned above whose eyes were miraculously healed has no doubt about the healing power of her Lord.

Who has believed our report? And to whom has the arm of the LORD been revealed?... We hid, as it were, our faces from Him; He was despised, and we did not esteem Him.

Surely He has borne our griefs and carried our sorrows; yet we esteemed Him stricken, smitten by God, and afflicted. But He was wounded for our transgressions, He was bruised for our iniquities; the chastisement for our peace was upon Him, and by His stripes we are healed. (Isaiah 53:1, 3–5)

I'm a bit puzzled even by the Bible translators, who apparently didn't believe Isaiah's report! All they could see was the payment for sin without the payment for sickness, so they translated two key words in verse 4 in the above passage as *"griefs"* and *"sorrows"* instead of "sickness" and "pain." However, Matthew 8:16–17 makes it clear that healing was in the atonement, because it says,

When evening had come, they brought to Him [Jesus] many who were demon-possessed. And He cast out the spirits with a word, and healed all who were sick, that it might be fulfilled which was spoken by Isaiah the prophet, saying: "He Himself took our infirmities and bore our sicknesses."

Sickness Has Been Sent Away

Isaiah 53:5 says, *"He was wounded for our transgressions"*—the sins we commit against people—and *"He was bruised for our iniquities"*—the sins we commit against God. When you were born again, you realized Jesus took your place and was punished for all your sin, but did you understand that He carried it all *away?*

In showing you what Jesus did with sin, I want to show you what Jesus did with sickness. Jesus carried away your transgressions and your iniquities so that you would not have them anymore. Are you supposed to go back into your past and pick up the burden and guilt of your various sins? Does the Holy Spirit come to remind you of your sins? "You smoked," "You took drugs," "You lied," or whatever? Of course not! The Holy Spirit comes to set you free and to let you know that your sin has been carried away *"as far as the east is from the west"* (Psalm 103:12).

In the Old Testament, there is a very graphic picture of what God did with sin. Leviticus 16:7–22 contains God's instruction concerning what is called the "scapegoat." Once a year, on the Day of Atonement, two goats were brought to the door of the tabernacle when the sin of the people was to be purged. Lots were cast to choose which goat was to be presented before the Lord and which goat was to be driven into the wilderness, or desert.

The first goat was killed, and its blood was taken into the Holy of Holies, where it was sprinkled on the mercy seat, signifying the covering of the people's sin. Then, the priest laid his hands on the living goat, confessing over the "scapegoat" all the iniquities and transgressions of the Israelites. This goat, "carrying all the sin," was led into the wilderness, where it was released, thus signifying that the people's sin was carried away to a place where it would never be seen again. In this manner, the Lord not only purged the sin of His people, but He also *put it away.*

What a wonderful picture of what Jesus did for us at Calvary. When He died, He took the punishment each of us deserved because of sin. However, that is not all that He did; He *carried away* all our sin. Do you see that Jesus was represented by both goats in the Old Testament? He is our "scapegoat." Jesus not only forgave your sin, but He also set you *free* from your sin. The past has been forgiven and forgotten! You don't have to fear that your sin is suddenly going to jump on you, because it has been driven into the sea of God's forgetfulness. (See Micah 7:19.)

Through Christ, you have been born again and given a new nature so that you can live freely in His life rather than living under the bondage of sin and death. (See Romans 8:2.) A sin nature no longer rules your life, because you have made Jesus your Lord. Does that mean you can never sin again? No, your freedom of choice is never removed; but your desires have been changed. I knew an evangelist who would shock his audiences by saying, "I smoke all I want, I drink all I want, I lie and cheat all I want." With a remark like that, he certainly got everyone's attention; then, he would quickly add, "I just don't want to do any of those things!"

> *But if we walk in the light as He is in the light, we have fellowship with one another, and the blood of Jesus Christ His Son cleanses us from all sin....If we confess our sins, He is faithful and just to forgive us our sins and to cleanse us from all unrighteousness.* (1 John 1:7, 9)

You may say, "I know all this regarding sin, but how does it relate to sickness?" Jesus not only took

Jesus took sin and sickness upon Himself in order that you might walk free of sin and free of sickness. That is truly divine health.

the punishment and paid the price for sickness as well as for sin, but He also carried sickness away in the same package with sin, so that you wouldn't have to suffer from either again. Jesus is your "scapegoat" for sickness, too. The Old Testament scapegoat was driven so far into the wilderness that it never made its way back into the Israelites' camp, and neither is sickness supposed to come back upon you. Jesus *carried sickness away* along with your sin. Jesus took sin and sickness upon Himself in order that you might walk free of sin and free of sickness. That is truly divine health.

What do you conspire against the LORD? He will make an utter end of it. Affliction will not rise up a second time. (Nahum 1:9)

Just as the Lord has made provision for sin committed by believers, He has made provision for the physical ills of believers. Over and over in the Old and New Testaments, God has given us promises for the healing of our bodies. We should all be growing in the knowledge of the Lord, and that *knowledge contained in the Word* gives us greater and greater power to live a sinless life in a healthy body. However, we must exercise that power. Change your mind about sickness! Change what you say about sickness! Don't just expect to be healed if you are ill; expect to walk in health. You have the nature of the One who is *never sick*, just as surely as you have the nature of the One who *never sins*.

The apostle Paul prayed that *"the God of our Lord Jesus Christ, the Father of glory,* [might give to us] *the spirit of wisdom and revelation* **in the knowledge of Him"** (Ephesians 1:17). Paul wanted every believer to understand clearly the good things that God has in mind for His children, and how many benefits and blessings He has laid up in store for us. Among these benefits are healing and health. Praise the Lord, Paul didn't stop there. He continued by emphasizing God's ability and power to give all these blessings to us, ability and power that were demonstrated when He raised Jesus from the dead. That *same* power is working for all those who believe. (See verses 18–19.)

In case there may still be a question in your mind concerning whether healing is a part of the atonement, let me again take you to Matthew 8:16–17. This portion of Scripture describes a typical day in the life of the Lord Jesus. The people had brought many to Jesus who were either possessed by demons or who were sick in their bodies. Jesus cast out the demons with His word, and He healed *all* the people who were ill. Notice again what the Holy Spirit recorded next through Matthew: *"That it might be fulfilled which was spoken by Isaiah the prophet, saying: 'He Himself took our infirmities and bore our sicknesses'"* (verse 17). This verse clearly refers to Isaiah 53:4 and shows that Jesus, in fulfilling Isaiah's prophecy, is not only our Savior but also our Healer.

Without question, healing for our physical bodies is in the atonement.

In this account from Matthew, I want you to notice that faith in Jesus' ability to heal caused people to bring others who were sick and afflicted to Him for their healing. The people who needed a touch from Jesus did not come on their own. Many times in the Scriptures, the sick and oppressed were healed through the faith of someone else. If it happened then, it can happen today. We can stand in faith for another, even when that other person is not exercising faith. That may seem preposterous, but it is true. The centurion believed for his servant (see Matthew 8:5–10), Jairus believed for his daughter (see Mark 5:22–24, 35–43), and friends believed for the paralytic who was lowered through a roof into Jesus' presence (see Mark 2:1–12). God wants us well so much that He accepts the afflicted one's faith or the faith of another on his or her behalf.

Years ago, my mother traveled to Dallas, Texas, to hear a man who had a dynamic healing ministry. Mother was terribly burdened for my father, who had suffered a nervous breakdown and was in very bad shape. When my mother stood weeping before this evangelist, he received a word of knowledge about the situation. "You are crying because you think your husband is demon possessed," he told my mother, "but that is not the case." He said my father was terribly oppressed and broken down. Then, the man of God told my mother to take the handkerchief into which she had shed her tears and lay it on my father's body. My mother obeyed these unusual instructions, and my father began to mend. The last period of my father's life was the most victorious he had ever known.

This may sound strange to you, but just such oddities occur in the Scriptures. Don't forget that the Lord is always the same, and what He has done for one person, He will do for another. Do you recall the incident where God worked special miracles by the hands of Paul? Handkerchiefs or pieces of cloth were taken from Paul by the friends or relatives of people who were ill. When these cloths were given to the sick, they were healed of diseases and delivered from demonic activity. (See Acts 19:11–12.) Even the shadow of Peter apparently healed the sick and afflicted. (See Acts 5:15.) Don't limit God! His thoughts are not limited to our thoughts, and neither are His ways. (See Isaiah 55:8–9.) Open your heart and your mind to everything the Lord has for you.

Redeemed from the Curse of the Law

Previously, I pointed out that when sin entered the human experience, sickness came with it. It is only reasonable to conclude that when Jesus took care of the problem of sin, He also took care of the problem of sickness; they came in the same package. Sickness was the effect of sin. God warned His people in the Old Testament that sin brought sickness, but obedience brought health and healing. Again, Deuteronomy 27 outlines those things that come as a result of sin and then concludes, *"Cursed is the one who does not confirm all the words of this law"* (verse 26). The results of sin are what Paul called *"the curse of the law"* (Galatians 3:13). All manner of illness is

> *Christ redeemed you and me from everything related to the curse, and that includes sickness.*

mentioned in the Deuteronomy passage, as well as other calamities. As sinners, we were under the curse of the law. However, Jesus took the curse upon Himself at Calvary. (See Galatians 3:13.) Christ redeemed you and me from everything related to the curse, and that includes sickness.

The word *redeem* means "to buy back." Jesus bought us back when we were in the "slave market" of sin. He paid the price for the redemption of our lives with His own perfect life. The English word *redemption* comes from the Latin word for *redeem*. If I buy something, I have purchased it, and it then belongs to me. No one else can lay claim to what I have bought. However, *redeem* means much more than simply buying an object; it means "to repossess" that object through purchase.

Humanity originally belonged to God; we were His creation and His possession, created for His pleasure. Then, Adam's all-encompassing "error" gave the devil possession of something that truly wasn't his. Satan proceeded to misuse, abuse, and ruin God's perfect product until no one would want it but an ever-loving, compassionate Maker. God saw the possibility of restoring His creation to its original state and original condition. So, He set in motion a plan to "buy back" that which was so priceless to Him—but the price tag was His priceless Son. The transaction was completed at Calvary, where the Lord redeemed you and me and reinstated us as His own.

Let's see what God bought back:

Do you not know that your body is the temple of the Holy Spirit who is in you, whom you have from God, and you are not your own? For you were bought at a price; therefore glorify God in your body and in your spirit, which are God's.

(1 Corinthians 6:19–20)

Where does the Holy Spirit live, and where are you supposed to glorify God? In your body! Does the Holy Spirit want to live in a dump? Of course not. How can you glorify God in your body? There are several ways, but being well and staying well is of prime importance in giving God glory through your body. You are made in His image and likeness, so let the world see what God is like. Be healed!

Most Christians have no difficulty believing that they are redeemed in their souls as well as their spirits. But when it comes to physical redemption, many have a problem believing. However, it is only reasonable that redemption is for the whole person. You are a three-part being—spirit, soul, and body—and God intends for you to be like Him in every area of your being. I'm sure you want to glorify the Lord by demonstrating His likeness in your mind, in your spirit, and *in your body.*

One part of your being is no less important to the Lord than another. You have been redeemed in body as well as in spirit and soul. Whatever you

You have authority over sicknesses and diseases that attempt to invade your body or the body of another.

are going to do for God in this world is going to be done while you are in your body. Of course, every believer will receive a resurrected body at the resurrection—a body that will not be subject to corruption and death. (See, for example, 1 Corinthians 15:51–53.) In the meantime, the Lord has made provision for you to live in a body that can be healthy and strong. You have authority over sicknesses and diseases that attempt to invade your body or the body of another. Exercise that right and privilege. (See Luke 10:19.)

Once, a couple in our church took a transient into their home because he had no place to go. When the young man became ill, the couple sent him to the doctor. To their dismay, tests revealed that the young man had AIDS. Anger boiled in the heart of the man who had so graciously given a home to an individual who now seemed to threaten the health and even the lives of his family members. This man's first thought was to order his "guest" out of the house.

Before the man could say anything, the Holy Spirit spoke in his heart, telling him to spend his anger on the disease and not on the young man who was so ill. Forcefully, and with authority, the man commanded AIDS to leave the house and never return. Many months and several tests later, there was no sign of AIDS in the young man's body. Why?

Because Jesus paid the price for his healing, and one man exercised his authority in Christ!

Isn't Jesus the Word made flesh? (See John 1:14.) Well, Psalm 107:20 says that God sent His Word and healed you. Jesus assuredly paid for your physical body with His own physical body in the work of redemption. He said that He would die in your place for your sins, and He carried away those sins. He said that He would take stripes on His back for your sicknesses. Not only did He carry away your sins, but He also carried away your sicknesses. When the Word says God did something, it was obviously His will to do it. Therefore, I know it is the will of God to heal our bodies. Otherwise, Jesus would not have taken those stripes for our healing.

I've heard people say that even though God is willing to heal, it is obvious that not all people get healed; so, in some cases, God must have a reason for not healing. To substantiate their argument, they may say that God is not willing for anyone to perish, but we know there are people perishing every day. That's right, but did Jesus pay the full price for sin so that not one soul should ever have to go to hell? Yes, He did—so, that isn't God's choice; it's an individual's choice, through rejecting that provision.

Jesus paid the full price for your healing, and God wants you to take it. He doesn't want you to be ignorant about what is yours in Christ. He wants you to receive what is yours by choosing to accept it.

I want to share a testimony in which a choice made the difference. A woman wrote and told me how the Lord had healed her body as a result of her watching my TV program. At the point where I prayed for the sick, she thought, *Why not!* She prayed with me, laying her hands on the area of her back and kidneys where she was suffering severe pain. In her own words, "No one this side of heaven could ever know how badly I hurt for ever so long." The constant pain persisted even after prayer, but this woman continued to stand on her choice to be healed. When she awoke the next morning, all the pain was gone! The letter concluded, "Jesus must surely understand our hurts, and He shows compassion. I thank Him for taking all that pain on Himself." Praise the Lord, this woman's healing was just a choice away.

Why does God want to heal His people, and how has He demonstrated that willingness? Undoubtedly, the best expression of the Father's will is seen in the life of Jesus. But God didn't wait until Jesus ministered healing to tell His people why He wants them to be healthy in body. Although there are words and "pictures" throughout the Old Testament that express God's desire to heal, Micah 7:18–19 wonderfully sums up the reason:

> *Who is a God like You, pardoning iniquity and passing over the transgression of the remnant of His heritage? He does not retain His anger forever, **because He delights in mercy. He will again have compassion on us**, and will subdue our iniquities. You will cast all our sins into the depths of the sea.*

Pictures of Jesus as Redeemer-Healer in the Old Testament

Our God is merciful and compassionate. Illness, for any reason, does not please Him. It never delights the Lord to see His people sick. He delights in mercy, and His compassion for us causes Him to take action. God took action first in the garden of Eden when He slew an animal, sprinkled its blood, and covered Adam and Eve. (See Genesis 3:21.) I know the Bible doesn't say the animal was a lamb, but I believe it was, because that sacrificed animal was the first "picture" we have of Jesus, the Lamb who was sacrificed for us.

In every Old Testament feast or religious ordinance, a picture of Jesus can be found. Here are several of them.

In the Passover Lamb

Let's look again at the events concerning the Passover, in which Jesus was beautifully portrayed in the Passover lamb. When a "perfect" lamb without a spot or blemish was killed for each family in Israel, it wasn't just the blood that brought about deliverance. Again, although that blood on the doorposts caused the death angel to pass over those homes, I believe it was the lamb the people ate that healed every sick and feeble person among them. In Psalm 105, in a description of God's deliverance of the Israelites from Egypt, we read this statement: *"He brought them forth also with silver and gold: and there was not one feeble person among their tribes"* (verse 37 KJV). Jesus, our "Passover Lamb," is both Savior and Healer.

In the Cleansing of Lepers

Another Old Testament picture of Jesus is found in the cleansing of lepers. Even in those days, lepers could be healed. It wasn't medically possible, but it was possible with God. The healed leper would bring two birds to the priest, who would kill one bird. When the living bird was dipped in the blood of the dead bird, it would be released to fly away. Then, with some of the blood and oil, the priest would "anoint" the leper's right ear, thumb, and big toe. After this procedure, the priest would pronounce the leper clean. Once again, we see Jesus pictured in the two birds; in death He shed His blood for our sin, but He also carried away that sin.

In the Bronze Serpent

One of the most graphic pictures of Jesus and His redemptive work at Calvary is seen in the bronze serpent that Moses lifted up on a pole in the midst of the Israelites. (See John 3:14–15.) Did looking at that serpent forgive sins, or did it heal bodies? It healed bodies! I do believe God forgave the people for their murmuring when they were willing to look at the bronze serpent, but the purpose of the serpent was to effect healing in those who had been bitten by poisonous snakes.

A Better Covenant

Repeatedly in the Old Testament, God demonstrated His mercy and compassion by healing people. God is telling us through these examples that He wants people whole in body as well as in spirit, because He loves and cares for everyone. Then, *"when the fullness of the time had come, God sent forth His Son, born of a woman, born under the law, to redeem those who were under the law"* (Galatians 4:4–5). Although Jesus was completely human, He was also completely divine, an exact representation of the Father. The Scriptures tell us, *"The Son is the radiance of God's glory and the exact representation of his being"* (Hebrews 1:3 NIV), and *"In Christ all the fullness of the Deity lives in bodily form"* (Colossians 2:9 NIV). The character and ways of the Father were demonstrated in everything the Son did. As I mentioned earlier, many times, the Word says that Jesus ministered to people's needs because He was moved with compassion. Since Jesus was moved with compassion, we know that the Father was, also, and the Holy Spirit in Jesus fed hungry stomachs, *healed sick bodies*, and raised the dead.

Although wholeness and healing for the body were nothing new with the coming of a new covenant, the new is better. Whatever benefits and privileges belonged to God's people in the old covenant, we now have in a greater and more perfect dimension because we no longer look for a Redeemer in types and shadows. We now see Jesus clearly, the One who made the ultimate sacrifice through the

> *Whatever benefits and privileges belonged to God's people in the old covenant, we now have in a greater and more perfect dimension.*

shedding of His own blood. Before Jesus' death and resurrection, sin was only covered; but when Jesus "signed" a new testament with His blood, sin and sickness were put away. If the old covenant had been the best, there would have been no need for a better one. *"For if that first covenant had been faultless, then no place would have been sought for a second"* (Hebrews 8:7).

If God healed in the Old Testament, is He going to heal in the New Testament? Obviously, the answer is yes. If God healed in the New Testament, is He going to heal today? Hebrews 13:8 reveals Jesus as the One who is the same yesterday, *today,* and forever. Therefore, Jesus is healing today, and He will continue to heal as long as there are sick bodies to heal. If the God of the old covenant healed because of mercy and compassion, He is healing today because of mercy and compassion. How do I know? Again and again, the book of Psalms and other Scriptures declare that God's mercy endures forever:

> *Oh, give thanks to the LORD, for He is good!*
> *For His mercy endures forever.*
> (Psalm 136:1)

> *Praise the LORD of hosts, for the LORD is good,*
> *for His mercy endures forever.*
> (Jeremiah 33:11)

> *Through the Lord's mercies we are not consumed, because His compassions fail not.*
> *They are new every morning; great is Your faithfulness.* (Lamentations 3:22–23)

Moved with Compassion

Compassion moved Jesus to heal the sick and deliver those who were demonized. The main Greek word translated "*compassion*" in the Gospels means "to be deeply stirred or moved from within." Quite literally, Jesus was *moved* with compassion. When Jesus healed the leper who fell at His feet begging to be healed, the plight of the man caused Jesus to be moved with compassion, and He expressed His will by healing the man. (See Mark 1:40–42.) I must add that the man had faith to be healed. If God's compassion were the only requirement for healing, every person alive would be well and healthy. Yet, if we have the faith, God always has the compassion.

It isn't difficult for people to have compassion on those who are sick. But when individuals demonstrate demonic activity, people are more often moved with fear or disgust rather than by compassion. However, this was never Jesus' response to the demonized; He always responded with compassion. After delivering the man of Gadara who had a legion of demons, Jesus told him to go home to his friends and tell them of the great thing the Lord had done for him because He'd had compassion on him. (See Mark 5:19.)

Jesus was moved with compassion when He saw the weary multitudes who were scattered like sheep without a shepherd. (See Matthew 9:36.) Jesus' compassion moved Him to heal the sick among those multitudes of people (see verse 35), and compassion moved Him to feed a hungry crowd more than once (see, for example, Mark 6:34–44). The compassion of our Lord caused Him to give sight to two blind men from Jericho (see Matthew 20:29–34), and compassion for a widow who had lost her son caused Jesus to stop a funeral procession and raise the young man from the dead (see Luke 7:11–16).

Many times, the writers of the Gospels recorded the compassion of Jesus that moved the Lord to continually minister deliverance to those oppressed by sickness and demons. Jesus Himself, in telling the story of the prodigal son, emphasized the compassion of this young man's father in welcoming him back home and reinstating him to the position of son and heir, which the prodigal had forfeited. (See Luke 15:20.) Do you realize that Jesus is illustrating the love of our heavenly Father for His wayward children? Without the anointing of the Holy Spirit, Jesus could have healed no one; so, obviously, the Holy Spirit is just as compassionate as both the Father and the Son. I believe compassion is the "emotion" of love that activates God's love.

Does God want His compassion to flow through you just as it flowed through Jesus? Absolutely.

Does God want His compassion to flow through you just as it flowed through Jesus? Absolutely. If you do not have compassion for people, then you are not going to be effective in ministering to others. Jesus spoke to *every* believer when He said,

Most assuredly, I say to you, he who believes in Me, the works that I do he will do

also; and greater works than these he will do, because I go to My Father. (John 14:12)

Look at this! The same Holy Spirit who empowered Jesus has come to reside in you, and He is able to perform even greater works through the members of Christ's body—when we are moved with His compassion.

For you had compassion on me in my chains, and joyfully accepted the plundering of your goods, knowing that you have a better and an enduring possession for yourselves in heaven. (Hebrews 10:34)

All of you be of one mind, having compassion for one another; love as brothers, be tenderhearted, be courteous. (1 Peter 3:8)

Seldom have I ever been more deeply touched with compassion than when I looked at the arms of a sixteen-year-old Russian girl. I felt as though my heart would tear out of me when I learned of the "mis"-fortune that had befallen Natasha. Both her arms were horribly scarred where obscenities and blasphemies had been carved by demons. Yes, demons! Natasha's mother had invited Gypsy fortune-tellers to read their "fortunes," and from that time, the writings were painfully cut into Natasha's arms by invisible personalities. A young man, *moved with compassion* for Natasha, brought her to one of my first meetings in Russia.

When Natasha heard the good news of salvation, she gave her heart to Jesus. In the authority

of Jesus' name, we bound the spirits that were using those precious arms for tablets and commanded
that they never do so again. The next time I went
to Russia, I was met by a lovely young woman who
handed me a beautiful bouquet of flowers. Yes, it was
Natasha. She held out both arms, and I saw that
there was little evidence of the awful cuts. The Lord
had not only healed her arms, but He had also delivered her from the demons. I've seen Natasha several
times since then, and she is living her life for the
Lord Jesus Christ. My husband, Wally, says that we
came close to having another child. Because I was so
moved with love and compassion for this young girl, I
could easily have brought her home with me.

The Anointing Breaks the Yoke

I have noticed that healing always comes by the
power of the Holy Spirit:

> *God anointed Jesus of Nazareth with the
> Holy Spirit and with power, who went
> about doing good and healing all who were
> oppressed by the devil, for God was with
> Him.* (Acts 10:38)

The Father heals because He is merciful and
compassionate, and the Son heals because He does
what the Father does. However, as I mentioned briefly before, Jesus doesn't heal just by the Father's love
and compassion; He heals by the *anointing.* The Word
reveals that Jesus didn't heal the sick until after He
was anointed with the Holy Spirit. (See, for example,
Mark 1:10–12, 23–34.)

Jesus was endued with power from the Spirit of God; that power or anointing was what healed and delivered. Did you know the Father promised the same anointing for those who are born again? Jesus, referring to this anointing as the baptism with the Holy Spirit, commanded that every believer receive it. (See Acts 1:4–5, 8.) That anointing came for the first time on the day of Pentecost. (See Acts 2:1–4.) Peter afterward declared that the same experience is for us, for our children, and *"to all who are afar off, as many as the Lord our God will call"* (verse 39).

The anointing brings healing because it breaks the yoke of Satan's bondage:

> *And it shall come to pass in that day, that his burden shall be taken away from off thy shoulder, and his yoke from off thy neck,* **and the yoke shall be destroyed because of the anointing.** (Isaiah 10:27 KJV)

The apostle Paul was very much aware that it was the anointing that gave him the power to accomplish anything for God. In Romans 15:17–19, he carefully gave the Spirit of God credit for any and all of the mighty signs and wonders that were manifested through him as he preached the gospel.

God always wants to confirm His Word with healing and deliverance, products that serve as evidence of the power and anointing of the Holy

> *God always wants to confirm His Word with healing and deliverance.*

Spirit. The Lord yearns for you to receive His anointing; He wants to work miracles through your hands. He has promised believers that they shall lay hands on the sick, and the sick shall recover. Quoting Jesus, Mark wrote,

> *And these signs will follow those who believe: In My name they will cast out demons; they will speak with new tongues; they will take up serpents; and if they drink anything deadly, it will by no means hurt them;* **they will lay hands on the sick, and they will recover.** (Mark 16:17–18)

The anointing of the Holy Spirit does much more than heal bodies, as the above Scriptures attest. It breaks every yoke and enables us to walk not only in health, but also in full vigor. I continually confess that, according to Romans 8:11, the Spirit of Him who raised up Jesus from the dead dwells in me, and He who raised Christ from the dead is quickening, or giving life to, my mortal body by His Spirit who dwells in me. There is nothing quite so valuable as personalizing the promises of God.

Once, at a series of meetings where I was speaking, I really needed the quickening and invigorating power of the Holy Spirit in my body, and I was ever so grateful for that promise. The evangelist who held the meetings is a very vibrant man who enjoys fellowship. After the first evening meeting, which lasted until 11:00 p.m., I intended to refresh my body with a good night's rest since I was the morning speaker. However, a time of food and fellowship was planned for after the service, and I didn't retire until after 2:00 a.m.! A time of fellowship was planned for the ministry people between each of the services, and I thought I was being "revived to a rag," one of my husband's favorite expressions.

I looked around at the rest of the people and thought, *Isn't this getting to them?* But they looked and acted refreshed, and I realized I was being refreshed, as well. The Holy Spirit was quickening my mortal body. Now, I don't recommend that anyone "burn the candle at both ends"; proper rest is part of taking care of the body. However, in the fellowship of the Holy Spirit and in the midst of ministering under the anointing, we had all been refreshed rather than exhausted. The Lord will sustain you physically in all kinds of situations and circumstances when necessary. He will quicken your mortal body.

Jesus Wants to Heal You

We've seen that Jesus healed all manner of sickness among the people because of compassion and because of the anointing. However, the religiously "pious" objected because He didn't do it in the "right" way; He healed on the Sabbath. Does sickness take a day of rest? I've never noticed that it does. People come to church sick and hurting—and Jesus heals them! I have found seven places in the Gospels where Jesus healed on the Sabbath: He healed the man who was an invalid at the pool of Bethesda (see John 5:1–9 NIV), the man born blind (see John 9:1–14), the demoniac in Capernaum (see, for example, Luke 4:31–37), Peter's fevered mother-in-law (see Matthew 8:14–15), the man with the withered hand (see, for example, Mark 3:1–5), the woman who was bent over (see Luke 13:10–13), and the man with dropsy (see Luke 14:1–4). No matter who you are or where you are, Jesus wants to heal you. It doesn't matter if you have a common cold or terminal cancer, Jesus wants to heal you. Our Lord shows no partiality to people or to diseases. (See Acts 10:34–35.) You don't have to be a preacher or a Sunday school teacher or give half your income to the church to get ready for healing. You just have to believe that He has enough love, enough compassion, and enough power to do it for you. In Jesus' day, the people accepted healing, but those who were "religious" didn't believe He could forgive sin. Today, people believe He can forgive sin, but they question His healing power. Why not accept both? It's not only scriptural, but it's also being proven in the lives of men, women, boys, and girls every day.

One day, on the outskirts of Jericho, a blind man came to Jesus for the restoration of his sight. However, before he came, he *overcame* several obstacles. The man was just one in a multitude of people; would Jesus see Him? When the man called to Jesus, those around him told him to "shut up"; would Jesus hear him? The man wore a brightly colored robe that identified him as a blind person and gave him the right to beg for a living; would he throw away his "security blanket" and reach out to Jesus for a new life of faith and wholeness? The answer to all those questions was yes, and Bartimaeus received his healing that day. (See Mark 10:46–52.) Today, I want you to lay aside all the obstacles in your life and circumstances that hinder you, and believe Jesus. He will heal you if you need healing, and He will use you in healing others. *You* can have His compassion, and *you* can have His anointing!

5

God Is Love

The love bug will bite you if you don't watch out!"
Have you ever heard that old tune, which was a
popular hit many years ago? It was a lighthearted
little jingle about love and romance, but the truth it
conveyed is as old as humanity. If nothing else will
get to you, love will. Love has changed the course of
history; kings have given up their thrones for the love
of their ladies; warriors have died on the battlefield
for the love of country; courageous men, women, and
children have given up their lives for people whom
they loved; even animals have performed heroic feats
to rescue beloved masters. Love is the most powerful
force on earth. *God is love!*

I was so touched by the testimony of a woman who was healed in one of our church services.
This woman had had three major things wrong with
her back, but she had never reached out with any
confidence to receive healing. Why hadn't she done

this when she attended a church where healing was preached and where people were prayed for in nearly every service with great results? I'll tell you why. The enemy had convinced this woman that her back would never be healed because she was not "worthy" to receive healing.

That old lie makes me so angry! I want to get up and punch the devil in the nose. However, we do not wrestle with flesh and blood but with principalities and powers in the spirit realm. (See Ephesians 6:12.) We have a weapon that will whip the devil every time, and that weapon is the Word of God. The evening the woman was healed, I was teaching on the love and compassion of God to heal. As the lady *heard* God's love letter to her, faith and confidence rose in her heart, and she reached out to Someone who loved her, Someone who had covered her with His worthiness—and she was healed. Oh, the love of God is so powerful! I'll tell you, that evening the devil did get a "bloody nose."

The Love of God Is Powerful

I believe that every person, at some time in his or her life, wonders who God is and what He is like. Civilizations around the world have "worshipped" an ugly, ferocious god who is vindictive and cruel, or a god who plays with people like chess pieces, or a god who is totally uninterested in his creation. Some societies have imagined many, many gods; and some have deified dogs, cats, snakes, and even *flies*. The most twisted lie is that *each person is "god."* What a case of mistaken identity!

If none of these things is true, then what is God really like? Is it possible to actually know His nature, His essence, His character? Since no man has seen God at any time (see John 1:18; 1 John 4:12), how can we discover who and what God is? The only way is to know what God says about Himself. God says that He is love. God the Holy Spirit inspired the apostle John to pen these words:

> *Beloved, let us love one another, for love is of God; and everyone who loves is born of God and knows God....God is love, and he who abides in love abides in God, and God in him.* (1 John 4:7, 16)

We often say that God is power or that God is healer or that God is provider. Not really; God is love, and out of His love come power, healing, and provision. Out of God's love came creation and every other thing that He has ever done or ever will do. All these things describe the acts of God, but His character is love. The facts that God is eternal, omnipotent (all powerful), omnipresent (everywhere present), and omniscient (all knowing) describe the "what" of God, but love describes the "who" of God. Oh yes, God is all these other things, but they are all summed up in love.

Out of God's love come power, healing, and provision.

Since God is love, it is impossible for you not to be loved by Him. Just as surely as God exists, His love is being poured out on you. Right now, you may think there are certainly many things getting in the way of God's love, but I want you to know that God's love for you penetrates any barrier. There are no obstacles too big for the love of God. His love is constant, intense, and irrevocable. God loves sinners; God loves saints. He loves you when you are productive and when you are unproductive; He loves you when you are living victoriously and when you are living in defeat. God loves you unconditionally!

God is not like Santa Claus; His gifts are for you when you are "bad" and when you are "good." There is no doubt that faith in a righteous heart is more active than faith in a guilty heart; but in whatever condition an individual finds himself or herself, it is our loving God's desire to heal. Jesus paid the price for our healing, and God would be unjust if He did not heal each one who believes for healing.

I previously said there are no barriers to God's love, but you and I can put up barriers that rob us of our healings. I challenge you to discover any of your own personal barriers to God's healing work. The woman who finally received healing in her back had a barrier of feeling unworthy. Yet that hindrance melted in the warmth of God's love.

If you are a parent, you want your children to be healthy. When they are sick, you never want them to get sicker. You do everything in your power to bring about healing. You take them to the doctor; you give them prescribed medicine; you do whatever is necessary. Parents love their children and want no calamity to overtake them. Again, loving parents would rather be sick themselves than see their children sick. Most parents would take their child's sickness upon themselves, if that were possible. That is exactly what Jesus did; He took our sicknesses upon Himself, and then He carried them away.

Are you thinking that the Father did exactly the opposite when He put our sicknesses upon His Son Jesus? Don't forget that Jesus and the Father are One. They share divinity, and They shared in purchasing healing for Their children. Whatever Jesus suffered for you and me to pay the price for healing, the Father suffered, also. Although Jesus is the One who came from the Father, the Trinity endured the pain and the agony of the cross "together." I know it grieved the Father to turn His back on Jesus, and it grieved the Holy Spirit when He had to leave Jesus at His death. (See, for example, Mark 15:34.) They were in that thing together!

Ways Through Which God Heals

God is so intent on healing us and making us whole that He has a myriad of ways to do it. In the Scriptures, I've found fifteen different ways in which God heals. Why does He use so many different ways to heal? Wouldn't only one way be better? Although one way might seem simpler, I may have the answer to the question. If God healed in only one fashion, somebody would say, "Well, I just don't believe God heals that way," and he would miss out. For example, if healing came only through the anointing with oil, someone might say, "That's a Presbyterian way, and I'm not Presbyterian."

If God healed only through prayer cloths, there would be those who considered that to be the

Pentecostal way. If healing came only by speaking the Word, that might leave out everyone but the Baptists. Don't misunderstand; I'm not saying these methods of healing are limited strictly to the groups I mentioned, or that everyone in those groups has exactly the same outlook, but I am making a point. We are all so varied in our personalities, backgrounds, and experiences that God meets us whatever we are. God is certainly not limited in the methods He uses to heal.

> *God is not limited in the methods He uses to heal.*

Let's not put a limit on God's healing ability. He says, in effect, "If My children can't receive anointing, then maybe they will receive the Word; if they can't receive the laying on of hands, then maybe they will receive a prayer cloth or some other method." In any case, the Lord "bends over backwards" to find a way in which we will receive His healing power. I'm convinced that when any person understands the love of God, he or she is stripped of all arguments; and love will change the heart—and the body.

Let's look now at these ways through which God heals. While they overlap at times, and the presence and anointing of the Holy Spirit is always involved, each way is also distinct and worth noting.

The Anointing

The first manner of healing I want to discuss is "anointing." The Word tells us God anointed Jesus of Nazareth with the Holy Spirit and with power. After that anointing, Jesus *"went about doing good and healing all who were oppressed by the devil, for God was with Him"* (Acts 10:38). I looked up the word in the Greek that is translated *"oppressed"* in this verse and found that it means "to dominate or exercise lordship." When Jesus healed people, He exercised His authority over Satan's domination and "lorded it over" sickness.

When you are sick, you are being oppressed, or dominated, by illness, because in Acts 10:38, the Word says those whom Jesus healed were oppressed by the devil. If sickness was the oppression, or domination, of the devil when Jesus was here on earth, it is still the oppression of the devil. Remember, it was Satan who set sickness in motion in the first place. It was he who poisoned the mainstream of human life at the beginning. Sickness, infirmity, and disease of any kind are the oppression of the devil. They are *always* his work:

> *Inasmuch then as the children have partaken of flesh and blood, He Himself* [Jesus] *likewise shared in the same, that through death He might destroy him who had the power of death, that is, the devil, and release those who through fear of death were all their lifetime subject to bondage.*
>
> (Hebrews 2:14–15)

Jesus came to set at liberty those who were bruised because of Satan's bondage. Jesus Himself, after reading from the scroll of Isaiah, declared to the people in the synagogue at Nazareth that He was the One *"anointed"* to do this work (see Luke 4:18), and He proved it by healing all manner of sickness (see verses 40–41). If you are suffering in some area of your body, Satan is exercising lordship over you; if you have cancer, it is dominating you; if you have AIDS, that thing has you bound. But praise the Lord that the anointing breaks the yoke! (See Isaiah 10:27 KJV.) Jesus has the power to free anyone who is under the lordship of Satan because Jesus is *Lord*:

> *The Spirit of the Lord GOD is upon Me, because the LORD has anointed Me to preach good tidings to the poor; He has sent Me to heal the brokenhearted, to proclaim liberty to the captives, and the opening of the prison to those who are bound.* (Isaiah 61:1)

I have good news for you! Jesus has done all that the Word said He would do. Jesus, the anointed of God (the Christ), opened the prison doors and released those who had been taken captive in their bodies through sickness of any sort. The doors are still open; healing is available for you more than two thousand years later. Read 1 John 3:8, and you will find, *"For this purpose the Son of God was manifested, that He might destroy the works of the devil."* Jesus took lordship over sickness at Calvary when He loosened and broke the works of the devil. There's no doubt that sickness is still around, but its power has been broken, and Jesus is still healing bodies today.

As I wrote earlier, many believe that healing is not for our day. They say that the purpose of healing in Jesus' life and ministry was to authenticate His divinity; they say healing was one of the proofs that He was God. When faced with the fact of healing in the early church, these people say that healing power was manifested only through the original apostles because they walked with Jesus. Or, they say that the healing ministry was for the purpose of getting the church established.

I heard a young pastor and theologian tell how God had transformed his mind and his heart about healing. He called himself a "cessationist" because he had adamantly believed all miracles and healings had ceased. He had read everything he could to substantiate his opinion and keep his mind bolted shut. Then, this man accepted an invitation to speak at a meeting in a church where the pastor held the same opinion—he thought. The closed-minded man found himself sharing the podium with a certain well-known "fundamentalist" who had stepped mightily into the healing arena. He found himself a captive audience to this pastor's views—and his experiences. Up until this time, the "cessationist" had never seen a healing. Yet, that day, he not only heard the Word *in truth*, but he also saw the healing power of Jesus on an anointed man break the bondage of sickness. This pastor began telling everyone who would listen that Jesus is healing bodies today.

My Bible says that the *anointing* breaks the yoke. Jesus was able to heal because He was anointed with the Holy Spirit. It was the presence of God the Holy Spirit on Jesus who performed the healing work. Jesus is now in heaven with the Father, but He and the Father sent the Holy Spirit back to earth, and the Spirit has the same anointing to heal the sick. Look at Jesus' own words:

Heal the sick, cleanse the lepers, raise the dead, cast out demons. Freely you have received, freely give. (Matthew 10:8–9)

And I will pray the Father, and He will give you another Helper ["Comforter" KJV], that He may abide with you forever.
(John 14:16)

But you shall receive power when the Holy Spirit has come upon you; and you shall be witnesses to Me in Jerusalem, and in all Judea and Samaria, and to the end of the earth. (Acts 1:8)

As believers, we are Jesus' representatives, having the same anointing He had to exercise authority over sickness in the lives of others.

Since the Holy Spirit is here on earth representing Jesus, who is always the same, yesterday, today, and forever, I know that God is still healing people today. As believers, we, too, are Jesus' representatives, and that same anointing is here for us, enabling us to exercise authority over sickness in the lives of others. If God had removed His power to heal, He also would have had to remove His power to save, and I don't think anyone would buy that as having occurred.

There are some people who, although they acknowledge that healing is for today, believe that God sovereignly exercises His right to use sickness as a means for drawing people to Him. I don't want any of you to buy that line, either. Although I dealt with this issue earlier, it bears mentioning again here. This idea is such a subtle attack on the finished work of Calvary. If sickness could draw people to God and make them love Him more, then the entire world would know and love God. People everywhere are sick or have been sick with something or other, and I don't see them flocking to God because of sickness. I know of more people who *don't* love God because they've been told He puts sickness on people.

When I am sick, my body doesn't want to worship and praise the Lord. I don't feel like I have the energy to read my Bible and pray when I'm feeling sick, and I don't think I love God more when I'm sick. Yes, the spirit is truly ready, but the flesh is weak. (See Mark 14:38.) Do you get out of a sickbed, full of enthusiasm to go to your neighbor and share the love of Christ? Do you jump out of that bed on Sunday morning and say, "I can hardly wait to get to church"? Personally, I want to roll over and pull the covers over my head. Instead, however, I do get up, go to church, receive anointing, and walk out whole. Hallelujah!

One of our pastors received a note from a lady who shared a remarkable testimony of healing. At our church, we pray over prayer cloths, knowing that the Lord anoints them with His healing power. One of our members took a prayer cloth to her boss, who had been diagnosed with cancer, and the boss was completely healed of the disease! Although the woman's boss does not attend our church, she wanted to come and give this testimony. What broke the bondage of cancer in her body? It was the anointing.

Sending the Word

Another way that healing is ministered is by "sending" the Word. Psalm 107:20 says, *"He sent His word and healed them, and delivered them from their destructions."* I agree with the psalmist, who continued in verse 21, *"Oh, that men would give thanks to the LORD for His goodness, and for His wonderful works to the children of men!"* Just think, God loves us so much that He gave us His Word, and that Word has healing power. The Word has mighty creative force; with the word of His power, God spoke the worlds into being. (See, for example, Psalm 33:6–9.)

You can find several occasions in the Scriptures when Jesus didn't go to the sick; He simply spoke a word of healing, and the individuals were made well. Once, when Jesus was teaching in Cana, a nobleman from Capernaum came to Him and begged Him to go and heal his son, who was at the point of death. This situation was critical; time was of the essence. Instead of going to Capernaum, Jesus said, *"Go your way; your son lives"* (John 4:50). The father believed Jesus, went home, and found his son well—healed at the very moment Jesus sent His word to him.

Can you send God's Word to heal sick bodies today? Yes, God's Word has the same dynamic power to heal today as it has ever had. The first time I really took hold of this promise was when my mother was told she had a brain tumor. We were out of town when I received the news that X-rays indicated the growth. Fear tried to grip my mind; my mother was alone, and we weren't there to pray for her. I was desperate; I felt I had to do something. Then, the Holy Spirit brought to mind, *"He sent His word and healed them."*

Immediately, I formed a mental picture of that verse, like an arrow, piercing my mother's brain. Then, I saw the arrow strike a dark spot, and the thing just exploded. I declared my faith and believed that God's Word had delivered my mother from that devilish destruction. I called my mother when Wally and I returned home, and I asked her to go to the doctor for another X-ray. You know that whatever God does can be authenticated. This X-ray came back with no sign of a tumor on my mother's brain. Glory to God! I sent the Word, and it brought healing.

Praise the Lord, the Word never wears out or loses its power! At our church, we are continually sending the Word. Prayer warriors man a prayer line where the Word is sent into every situation that prompts a call. The ministry is also flooded with prayer requests through the mail, and our staff prays over each one, sending the Word to every need. On my TV program, I always send the Word to heal sick bodies.

How I wish I could share all the miraculous testimonies of healing we receive, but here is just one. A woman who was scheduled for surgery to remove a large ovarian cyst called our prayer line. A prayer warrior prayed with her. Before the surgery, she was reexamined, and the cyst was gone. She wrote back giving praise to the Lord for her healing.

Speaking the Word

Speaking the Word is another way in which healing comes; not sending the Word but *speaking* the Word. I've observed several evangelists who move in healing and miracles. They just say something like, "Be well, in Jesus' name," or "In Jesus' name, be whole," and the people are healed. Healing doesn't come because a person prays and begs forever. Jesus said prayers aren't answered because they are long or fancy. Unbelievers expect to be heard because they pray long prayers. (See Matthew 6:7.) Prayer that is answered contains faith and power—Word power.

> *Prayer that is answered contains faith and power— Word power.*

Did Jesus heal this way? Look with me at the fifth chapter of John. To the sick man at the pool of Bethesda, Jesus simply said, *"Rise, take up your bed and walk"* (verse 8). When the Lord asked the man if he wanted to be well, the man began to give all the reasons why he wasn't healed. I imagine that Jesus thought, *Spare me the details; I'm going to make you well.* Jesus didn't pray a lengthy prayer; He just spoke the Word, and the man got up and walked away. For thirty-eight years, the man had been carried to the pool, but when Jesus spoke only seven words, the man was healed in a fraction of a minute. It's wonderful to see the power of the Word.

On another occasion, a Roman centurion, considering himself unworthy to approach Jesus, sent Jewish elders to Him to ask if He might come and heal a servant who was desperately ill. This Roman officer loved Israel and had built a synagogue for the Jews. Jesus responded to the call, but before He reached the centurion's home, friends met the Lord with a message of such faith from the centurion that it caused Jesus to say, *"I say to you, I have not found such great faith, not even in Israel!"* (Luke 7:9). The centurion asked only that Jesus *"say the word"* (verse 7) and his servant would be healed! This man understood authority because he had soldiers under him who either obeyed or died. Believing that Jesus' word had such authority, He entrusted his beloved servant to the power of His word. What were the results? The servant was healed! (See verse 10.)

As a teacher in the body of Christ, I continually have the privilege of seeing the results of speaking the Word. I want to tell you, it's exciting to see people receive the Word when it is spoken. The Holy Spirit often shows me someone in the congregation who is being changed by the Word. I often feel faith come down in a certain part of a group, and, later, someone from that area will say he was healed as he responded to the Word that was spoken. It isn't only physical healing that takes place as a result of the spoken Word. I hear testimonies of finances being healed, marriages being healed, and relationships being healed. Anything that needs healing can be healed through the spoken Word.

The Love and Compassion of Jesus

Next, I want to mention the love and compassion of Jesus to heal. Since I have already discussed this topic in some detail, I won't spend much time on it here. However, that is not to lessen its importance. For me, the awareness of God's love is the foundation of everything I can believe or receive. I've said before that everything God has done for us comes out of His great love. Matthew 14:14 says, *"And when Jesus went out He saw a great multitude; and He was moved with compassion for them, and healed their sick."*

This incident happened at a time when Jesus had just suffered great personal grief and loss over the murder of John the Baptist. The Lord tried to separate Himself from the crowd, but when the people followed Him, He was so touched by their need that He set aside His own need and ministered healing to them. What a poignant picture of God's love. That same compassion is still at work in hearts and lives. It comes from God and fills His children, causing them to "touch" others with healing power.

Obedience to the Word

Obedience to the Word also brings healing. One day, Jesus told a man with a withered arm to stretch out that arm. The man might have exclaimed, "Stretch out my arm? Are You a lunatic? I can't stretch out this withered arm." Instead, the man obeyed Jesus' word, and, when he attempted to do as Jesus had commanded, the crippled arm was healed. (See Matthew 12:13.) Likewise, when

Jesus told the man at the pool of Bethesda to get up and walk, that must have sounded preposterous to a man who hadn't walked in thirty-eight years, but *"he picked up his mat and walked"* (John 5:9).

The people in wheelchairs whom I see healed make an effort to rise from their chairs when a healing word is spoken to them. It may not happen immediately, but obedience to the Word of God brings healing. Sometimes, the things God tells you to do may seem strange to your mind, but obedience is the key. What do you suppose the crowd thought when Jesus spit on some dirt, applied it to a blind man's eyes, and told him to go wash off the mud at the pool of Siloam? That man could have missed his healing by getting upset when "spitballs" were put on his eyes. However, he obeyed Jesus' word and regained his vision. *"But for you who revere my name, the sun of righteousness will rise with healing in its wings"* (Malachi 4:2 NIV).

Agreement

I get excited over the power of agreement to heal. The Word tells us, *"Though one may be overpowered by another, two can withstand him. And a threefold cord is not quickly broken"* (Ecclesiastes 4:12). Agreement releases tremendous power, and it is so encouraging when others stand with you on the Word of God. If you grow faint and discouraged, you need someone else to believe with you. Jesus gave us a wonderful promise in Matthew 18:19 when He said, *"If two of you agree on earth concerning anything that they ask, it will be done for them by My Father in heaven.*" Even one person praying for another with a healing promise puts two people in agreement, and God is always in agreement with His Word.

Prayer

Prayer is another God-given tool through which we can receive healing. Prayer is our means of communication with God at all times and in every situation. We don't have to be in church, we don't have to have someone else agreeing, and we don't have to have hands laid on us or be touched by a famous healing evangelist. We can just lift a prayer to the Father, and He hears and answers. He is just a prayer away. *"Listen to me! You can pray for anything, and if you believe, you have it, it's yours!"* (Mark 11:24 TLB).

One of the finest and most effective missionaries of our day was healed just kneeling in prayer. This man had suffered a nervous breakdown, and, at the age of forty, was sent home from the mission field after being given no hope of ministering again. However, in a year, he was better, so he went back to India and almost immediately had another collapse. He found a quiet retreat in the mountains, but, after three months of rest, he was worse instead of better.

One day, when this missionary was in prayer, the Lord spoke to him, saying, *I want you to win many of the intellectuals of India, because no one is doing this.* The man was perplexed, and he argued with God. At the moment, he wasn't capable of doing anything; and, if he were, he didn't have the background or training needed to reach the intelligentsia. Then, God asked this man if he was willing, and the man said, "Yes." That response brought a healing flow into the man's mind and body, and he was totally restored. This missionary continued to work in India for years, and God used him mightily.

Faith

It seems to me that the most powerful way of healing is through *faith.* The "faith message" is nothing new in this age; it is as old as God's message to humanity. The words of Hebrews 11:6 are as sure today as they were the day they were written: *"But without faith it is impossible to please Him, for he who comes to God must believe that He is, and that He is a rewarder of those who diligently seek Him."* If God has promised something, He is as good as His Word.

God has not only promised healing, but He has also paid for it. Therefore, if we ask and believe, it is ours. One must be sure of God's will and then be diligent in seeking that will. The best way I know to be convinced and diligent is to meditate on the Scriptures from the Word of God that speak specifically to your circumstance. Put the Word in your heart and speak it with your mouth, and it will change your situation; it *will* remove your sickness. Multitudes of people have removed "mountains" of difficulty by speaking and speaking and speaking the Word and believing it in their hearts. (See Mark 11:23.)

> *Put the Word in your heart and speak it with your mouth, and it will change your situation.*

Repeatedly, Jesus rewarded faith. As we have seen, a hemorrhaging woman, a Roman centurion, friends of a paralytic man, several blind people, a leper, and the woman who had a demonized daughter received what they needed for themselves or others because of their faith. In contrast, Jesus healed very few in His own hometown of Nazareth because of their unbelief. I knew a man who had a successful healing ministry for over half a century. He simply taught the Word until such a faith level was built in people that they received their healings. Although this man strongly believed in a miracle-working God, he said he would rather teach faith than work miracles because people can lose what they don't know how to keep.

The Name of Jesus

The name of Jesus also brings healing. In Acts 3:1–8, we find Peter and John approaching the temple by the gate called "Beautiful." Before they made their way through the gate, a man who had been crippled from birth begged them for money. This was the cripple's only means of support, and every day he was brought to the gate. Money couldn't heal the man, but the disciples had something that could. Peter said, *"Silver and gold I do not have, but what I do have I give you: In the name of Jesus Christ of Nazareth, rise up and walk"* (verse 6).

Peter and John didn't anoint the man with oil, and they didn't lay hands on him; they didn't pray a religious prayer. Peter simply spoke the name of Jesus and commanded the man to rise and walk. Is there power in that name? Indeed, there is. The man didn't stumble and gradually get to his feet; he jumped up and began to leap all over the place. The name of Jesus destroyed the lordship of Satan. Look at what Jesus said: *"Until now you have asked nothing in My name. Ask, and you will receive, that your joy may be full"* (John 16:24). It was our Lord Himself who gave us the authority to use His name. He told believers they would take lordship over demons and difficult circumstances; they would lay hands on the sick, and they would recover. (See Mark 16:17–18.)

The devil and his demons tremble at the name of Jesus. Some of Satan's human emissaries arrested Peter and John and *ordered* them to stop preaching *in that name.* Satan was furious because thousands were accepting Christ and the sick were being healed, all in the name of Jesus. When Peter and John were released, they went to the other believers and called a prayer meeting. Here's what they prayed:

> *Now, Lord, look on their threats, and grant to Your servants that with all boldness they may speak Your word, by stretching out Your hand to heal, and that signs and wonders may be done through the name of Your holy Servant Jesus.* (Acts 4:29–30)

After they prayed, the place where they were assembled was shaken by the power of God, and they were all filled with the Holy Spirit. Then, they went right back to the streets to preach and heal in Jesus' name. (See verse 31.)

The name of Jesus alone spared a man from being shot and killed. I heard this testimony some years ago. The man was a "big time" gangster when the love of God touched him and he was born again. He could no longer make a living in crime, so he started a successful real estate business. However, the mob set out to kill him. One day, a man bolted into his office, pulled out a gun, and aimed it at him. The former gangster had time only to cry, "Jesus!" At that name, the gun flew out of the assassin's hand, and he *fell* helpless to the floor. The mob never bothered the man again.

A Word of Deliverance

Many times, a word of deliverance brings healing. The "discerning of spirits," one of the nine gifts of the Holy Spirit listed in 1 Corinthians 12:10, often operates in conjunction with the word of deliverance in delivering the sick. Sometimes, you have to speak directly to Satan and the root cause of sickness before healing comes. Jesus rebuked the fever that Peter's mother-in-law was suffering from, and the fever left her. Jesus didn't pray or anoint with oil; He simply spoke a word of deliverance. When the Holy Spirit reveals a root problem of sickness, such as a "spirit of infirmity" or a "spirit of death," it can be rebuked and the individual set free from illness and oppression. The Holy Spirit may reveal that bitterness or unforgiveness has brought sickness. When the person is willing to forgive, a word of deliverance will bring healing.

A Word of Knowledge

Another wonderful way in which the Lord ministers healing is through a "word of knowledge." This is mentioned in 1 Corinthians 12:8 as another of the nine gifts of the Holy Spirit. Let me illustrate. As I mentioned earlier, when I teach in meetings, the Lord usually gives me a word of knowledge about the physical needs of many in the congregation. Once, while I was teaching on healing, the Lord let me know there were a number of people there with foot problems. Two notable healings took place when I prayed for those who responded to a call for prayer. One woman had a bone in her foot put back in place, and mobility was restored to a man's foot and ankle, which had been fractured several months earlier. Many others reported that they were instantly relieved of severe pain in their feet. I had no previous knowledge of these foot problems, but the Lord let me in on a bit of His omniscience. Why? Because He loved them and wanted to heal them.

The Lord isn't going to let you know things about people just because you are curious or nosy. God is not a "tattletale," but He will give you information through a word of knowledge that will enable you to minister or pray more effectively. Believe it or not, He will even give you needed information about yourself. The Lord let me know there was a certain food that was not good for me, so I stopped eating it. At my next physical checkup, the doctor told me I would be wise to avoid the very food that I had already eliminated from my diet. Do you believe the Lord is interested in even the seemingly small things that concern you? I do!

> *The Lord is interested in even the seemingly small things that concern you.*

There are examples in the Scriptures where we see a word of knowledge in operation. Elisha "knew" that if Naaman dipped in the Jordan River seven times, he would be healed of leprosy. There was nothing supernatural about dipping seven times; neither did the Jordan have any therapeutic powers. Elisha's natural mind would never have proposed such a solution, but it worked because *God* said it would. (See 2 Kings 5:1–14.) In another example, Isaiah first received "word" that King Hezekiah would be raised from his deathbed and live another fifteen years, and that a poultice of figs should be prepared. (See 2 Kings 20:1–7 NIV.) *"They did so and applied it to the boil, and he recovered"* (verse 7). Wow! Should we all start eating figs or plastering them on our bodies? Of course not. Isaiah had received a word of knowledge for the king that effected a miraculous cure.

Fasting with Prayer

Fasting with prayer is probably the most disciplined method of producing healing. The body is seldom comfortable when deprived of food. Setting aside time to pray when one could be eating requires determination. Nevertheless, the rewards are quite dramatic.

Matthew 17:14–21 relates how a man brought his epileptic son to Jesus' disciples in order that they might heal him, but they were unable to do so. Jesus rebuked these disciples for their *unbelief*; then, He delivered the boy. After Jesus cast the demon out of the child, He told His disciples, *"This kind does not go out except by prayer and fasting"* (verse 21). Notice that

Jesus obviously practiced what He preached; also notice that prayer combined with fasting *strengthens faith.* Fasting is not a sacrifice that twists the arm of God, so to speak; *fasting subdues our flesh and enables our spirits to hear the voice of God.* Wouldn't you rather live in the Spirit than in the flesh?

I received a triumphant testimony from a woman who had been delivered from a bad situation through fasting and prayer. She had found herself being drawn into a relationship with a married man. The flattering attention she received from him was very satisfying to her flesh, but she was also very frightened. As a Christian, this woman knew the relationship was wrong, but no matter how hard she tried, she didn't have the strength to end it. When she became desperate, this woman decided to fast and pray about the matter. After three days, she was able to walk away from the situation in God's strength. I would say she received *healing* for her soul. It wasn't easy, but God took her yielded will and added His power. That's true "will power"!

Early in my husband Wally's adult Christian life, a friend of his was admitted to a mental hospital. Wally was so burdened for the man that he decided to do something he had never done before. He fasted—for only one meal, but the Lord graciously honored my husband's obedience and faith. Very shortly, Wally heard that his friend had been released from the hospital and was having no more difficulty. Is there someone you know who has an "unshakable" illness, or is there a problem in your own life that has not surrendered to anything you have done? Set aside some time to fast and pray, meditate on the Word, and let your faith level rise to the place of deliverance and healing.

God's Presence

There is another way of healing that is just dynamite! In Luke 5:17, we read that the very presence of the Lord has power to heal. Jesus was teaching the Pharisees and teachers of the law who had come from everywhere to hear Him, *"and the power of the Lord was present to heal them."* Just how can we enter into the power and the presence of the Lord to receive healing? Psalm 22:3 says, *"But thou art holy, O thou that inhabitest the praises of Israel"* (KJV). Isn't that wonderful! God is so pleased with our praise that He just comes down to fellowship with us, and the holiness of His presence makes sick bodies whole.

Kathryn Kuhlman had an unusual healing ministry that was as baffling to her as it was to her audiences. She said she didn't know how or why God healed so many in her meetings. The believer and the unbeliever, the skeptic and the person full of faith, were healed—it didn't seem to matter. However, there was one powerful dynamic in those services. Miss Kuhlman spent hours each day caught up in worshipping and praising the Lord, whom she loved with all her being. When she walked onto a platform, she simply took her audience into that worship and praise, and the power of the Lord was present to heal. Moreover, that mantle seemed to have fallen on a young pastor who worked in Miss Kuhlman's ministry. This man didn't spend a long time teaching or preaching in healing services. Instead, he involved the people in praise and worship, and healing began to flow.

Years ago, a friend of mine took a real skeptic to one of Miss Kuhlman's meetings. This woman had suffered a severe neck injury in an automobile accident. A fractured bone in her neck had been replaced through surgery, but she still experienced severe pain and some immobility in one arm. That evening, the woman became a believer in God's healing power for today when she was healed just sitting there as a spectator. I'm so thankful that Christian woman was willing to swallow her pride and share the good news with my friend. This person has since experienced God's healing touch many times in very critical circumstances.

Anointing with Oil

Another means of healing is the anointing with oil. Anointing a person with oil was a common practice in the Old Testament among the Jews. God commanded that kings and priests be anointed with oil, and we have seen that lepers who were cleansed were anointed with oil. We know that oil signifies the presence of the Holy Spirit. In the New Testament, James wrote,

> *Is anyone among you sick? Let him call for the elders of the church, and let them pray over him, anointing him with oil in the name of the Lord. And the prayer of faith will save the sick, and the Lord will raise him up.*

> *And if he has committed sins, he will be for-*
> *given.* (James 5:14–15)

I remember a somewhat amusing incident in my own life that took place when our church was in its infancy. I was suffering from an ear infection that stubbornly resisted medication and prayer. At one point, when I was in severe pain, I called my mother for advice. She told me to put a drop or two of warm oil in my ear because that often relieved an earache. Because I didn't have the proper kind of oil in my home, I went to our church, which was not far away, for the bottle of oil with which we anointed members of our congregation when they were sick. I put a few drops of that oil in my ear. Do you know, that was the last of my earache? Then, I realized I had used the anointing oil in my ear. I don't believe it was any medicinal property in that oil that healed my ear; the oil in that bottle was consecrated for the purpose of anointing the sick. It had been used numerous times to heal other sick bodies, and that day it healed my sick body.

The Sovereign Work of God

Last, I want to mention the sovereign work of God. We simply can't put a formula on every person's healing. Some people are healed, and we just don't know what it was that brought about their healing. We know only that God healed them. Do you understand why the dead soldier who was thrown into the sepulcher containing Elisha's bones was raised to life? Yes, it seems that God's power, which was upon Elisha, still resided in those bones. However, no one expected the soldier to be revived, certainly not the soldier. Prayer wasn't offered for him, hands weren't laid on him, and no one anointed him with oil. Nevertheless, God raised that soldier from the dead. I believe he was a God-fearing man after that, don't you?

People traveling to Miss Kuhlman's meetings were healed on the buses, and others were healed walking into the auditoriums where the meetings were held. If I tried to come up with an answer or a formula for every healing, I would only be guessing. I don't have all the answers, and neither do you; but this one thing I do know: God loves *people.* He wants to make them well and whole in every way, and He will go to any means possible to manifest His loving grace in our lives. Let's use all the ways the Lord has given us to heal and be healed. Speak the Word, send the Word, believe the Word, anoint with oil, use Jesus' name, rebuke sickness, fast and pray—use them all. Live expectantly, and trust God to use His unlimited power and resources on your behalf at your request!

God loves people. He wants to make them well and whole in every way.

6

The Heart Mender

It was impossible, but I was seeing it with my own eyes. The picture of the two men arm in arm moved my heart in an unspeakable way. These two men were worlds apart, and yet a gesture of love had brought them together. I'm always surprised when a news magazine reports good news, but this story was obviously newsworthy. I want to tell you the story behind that picture, which involved a Jewish cantor and a former Ku Klux Klan member. It all began when the Klansman started sending filthy, evil notes to the cantor and also leaving sick messages on the cantor's answering machine because he was eaten up with hatred for all Jewish people.

Angry and frustrated, the Jewish man called the police to see if they had an answer to his dilemma. Although the man thought he knew who might be doing these terrible things, he couldn't prove it, and the law-enforcement officers could offer no solution. Then, the

Jewish man took the matter into his own hands; he started leaving messages on the Klansman's phone. However, these messages had a different tone to them. The cantor said that if the Klansman had lived in Nazi Germany when the Jews were being exterminated, he would have been exterminated right along with them because he was a cripple. The Nazis, in attempting to produce the "super race," had killed all those who were mentally or physically disabled. With just short phone messages, the Jewish man made an attempt to inform the "hater" that he was involved in something that was both cruel and inhuman.

Eventually, one evening, the angry Klansman called the Jewish cantor and asked why he was leaving the messages on his phone. Why, indeed! With as much kindness as possible, the cantor told the other man that he was caught in an awful lie and his heart was all wrong. "You are in something very evil that is going to destroy you," he said. He concluded the conversation by expressing concern over how the physically disabled man did his grocery shopping and asked if he and his wife could do the Klansman's grocery shopping that week. However, he refused the offer.

After a few more weeks and a few more kind messages, the Jewish man called and asked if his wife could prepare a meal to bring to the man. This time, he said, "Yes." However, before the cantor and his wife brought over the meal, the wife expressed a desire to buy the man a silver ring. They purchased the ring and took the lovely gift along with the meal. After they all ate together, the Jewish couple presented the man with the beautifully wrapped gift.

Overwhelmed by the couple's love and generosity, the Klansman viewed the contents of the small box; then, he removed from his finger a ring engraved with a German swastika and placed the new ring on his finger.

That former Ku Klux Klan member renounced the organization and began traveling our nation speaking to young people about the terrible dangers of hate groups and the lies that put hatred in people's hearts against others. This man's life was totally turned around by the love of someone he had hated, and the two men became the best of friends. When asked by the press to give an explanation for what had happened, the cantor replied, "My Jewish faith teaches that you should be kind to your enemies, so I decided to practice what I preached—and it worked!" This gracious Jewish man and his wife may not have known Jesus as their Messiah, but they practiced what the Word teaches, and the Word always works.

Your Heart Is a Treasury

Did you know that healing really begins in the heart? It's not just what you eat that determines whether you're healthy or sick, but also the inward attitudes or "weights" that you allow to take up residence in your heart. The contents of your heart— envy, anger, bitterness, cruelty, fear, depression, immorality, all manner of evil—affect your spirit, soul, and body. If you harbor anything in your heart that is contrary to the Word of God, it will eventually begin to eat away at you physically.

Your heart attitudes today determine your health tomorrow. Healing works from the inside out.

The root cause of most sicknesses and diseases is directly related to the attitudes of the heart. Your heart attitudes today determine your health tomorrow. If you can get your attitudes in line with the Word of God, you can totally turn your health situation around.

Healing works from the inside out. Jesus announced to a hurting, dying world that He was anointed by the life-giving Spirit of God to *"preach good news to the poor"* (Luke 4:18 NIV). All of us are poor and lacking unless there is a dynamic flow of God's Spirit in our lives. Jesus went right to the "heart" of the matter when, first of all, He said He came to *"heal the brokenhearted"* (verse 18). Why must healing power begin in the heart? Proverbs 4:23 gives the answer: *"Keep your heart with all diligence, for out of it spring the issues of life."* Out of your innermost being comes the response to any situation with which you will ever deal. Your tongue is "attached" to the contents of your heart; as you draw out those contents with your tongue, you guide yourself toward life or death.

For out of the abundance of the heart the mouth speaks. A good man out of the good treasure of his heart brings forth good things, and an evil man out of the evil treasure brings forth evil things.
(Matthew 12:34–35)

Death and life are in the power of the tongue,
and those who love it will eat its fruit.
(Proverbs 18:21)

Pleasant words are like a honeycomb,
sweetness to the soul and health to the
bones. (Proverbs 16:24)

These truths are awesome and attention getting. The issues of your life will either be health, prosperity, happiness, peace, and joy, or they will be sin, bad attitudes, hatefulness, sadness, despair, and death. If you are a good person, it is only because you have been storing good things in the treasury of your heart. What makes an evil person? The evil things that are stored in the heart. Jesus came to preach and teach good news. He Himself is the Word, and what He taught was good. Jesus, the Word, is our heart mender: His Word stored in our hearts will heal and transform our hearts and our lives. One day, Jesus asked a man why he called Him good. Jesus explained that only God is good. (See, for example, Luke 18:18–19.) Our Lord was telling the man that He was God, and that He was good. When God and His Word live in the heart, the heart can be mended and healed.

Every person in the world has had ample opportunity to store evil things in his or her heart. You hay have heard the expression, "Life doesn't deal from a straight deck." In other words, life isn't fair; it is stacked with disappointments, failures, lies, misconceptions, and catastrophes of every sort. All these things stored in the heart produce heartache.

God will remove the poverty of your heart and soul and bestow His riches there.

The Lord Jesus came to remove the heartache and bring wholeness to our hearts. Praise the Lord! He has the ability to pluck the junk out of your heart. He will remove the poverty of your heart and soul and bestow His riches there. Then, you must fill your heart with the exceedingly great and precious promises of God, which will provide *everything* you need for life and godliness. (See 2 Peter 1:3–4 NIV.)

Our newspaper carried a tragic article concerning a man who gave his mother a gun with which to kill herself. The man was on trial for being instrumental in his mother's death. Why did this man do such a horrible thing? Why did his mother kill herself? Because they both had believed a lie. This son *thought* he was doing a loving, merciful thing because he had believed a lie. The mother had been having some physical problems, and medical tests indicated there was cancer in her body. So, without waiting for further tests, this poor woman, who was unwilling to suffer and die with cancer, took her own life with the gun provided by her son. After her death, it was learned that there had been no cancer in the mother's body. Her son was acquitted, but how severely he must have judged himself. I shudder when I think of the grief and the guilt with which this man must have dealt. How he needed Jesus' love and forgiveness to heal his broken heart.

Love Never Fails

How many get sick and die early because they believe the lies of the devil? You know, it's like putting a gun to your head and shooting yourself. Satan is a liar and the father of every lie (see John 8:44); his purpose is to plant lies in every human heart, especially lies about God. He hopes that you will buy into his lies and never be changed by God's truth and love. If your heart is wrong, it is difficult to receive healing for your physical body. Again, bitterness, resentment, envy, unforgiveness, and guilt—all this kind of junk and garbage from hell—keep people from being able to receive healing. These things will cause anyone to hold back from God or to feel guilty before Him. Then, healing can't really flow, because the heart is full of other things. Instead, we need to believe Truth; God says He loves us and desires to give us a long and happy life. (See, for example, John 3:16; 10:10.)

"Love never fails" (1 Corinthians 13:8). Let me say it again: love never fails! A member of our church who is a hairstylist told me this amazing story of God's love. One evening, he came home from work and found his front door unlocked. Knowing that he never left the door unlocked and feeling that someone was in the apartment, he cautiously searched the rooms. When the man entered the bathroom, there was an intruder trying to hide in the bathtub. He was a large man, capable of overpowering my friend. However, a peace enveloped him, and he very calmly asked, "What are you doing in my apartment?"

The man in the tub replied that someone had been breaking into apartments on that floor, and he had chased the individual into that apartment. When he didn't find the burglar, he decided to stay and protect the apartment—in the bathtub.

Telling the man how very kind that was, my friend suggested they both go look for the burglar. After ushering him into the hall, he said they really should tell the manager, so together they went to the manager's office. The hairstylist said to the manager, "I found this man in my apartment; he says he was looking for a burglar, but I think *he* is the burglar." The man admitted it was true; he was the burglar. Praise the Lord, the man was caught before anything was taken, and no one was hurt. My friend told me that he had a gun in the apartment, but when he'd thought about getting it, the Lord had spoken to him and said, "Don't use the gun; use your love!"

We may easily accept the fact that God is love, but that fact can be very intimidating when we realize that God expects us to love as He loves. That may not be so easy. I can just hear someone saying, "Of course, God can love; He's God. But I'm not like that." Now, wait a minute! In whose image and in whose likeness are we all created? If we are made in God's image, who do we think we are like? God didn't make us like the devil; He made us like Himself. We see God's image in Jesus Christ, and when Jesus lives in our hearts, we *can* love as He loves. You and I were cut out of "God material," so we bear the mark, or stamp, of God's love—the love that *can* love and *wants* to love. Don't get the "can'ts"; get the "cans."

Two Natures at War

Even though human beings have a fallen nature, they have the remnants of their original, or primary, nature—the nature humanity was first given by God, the love nature. God said that nature was good because it was like Him. (See Genesis 1:26–31.) However, when Adam and Eve sinned, they became spiritually dead in sin (see Ephesians 2:1–2; Colossians 2:13), and they opened the door to a secondary nature that is not good. That secondary nature is a nature of sin and hate. So, human beings have an underlying primary nature, as well as a secondary nature, and the two are opposed to one another.

Before you accepted Christ, you knew that love could warm your heart, you enjoyed loving others, and it felt good to be loved. You were responding to your primary nature—God's stamp on your being—even though you weren't born again. Deep down, for most of us, it doesn't feel good to sin or to hate because God didn't make us that way.

Deep down, for most of us, it doesn't feel good to sin or to hate because God didn't make us that way.

Some people say it's "just our nature" to sin, so we can't keep from sinning. Yes, we have a sin nature, and all it can do is sin; but that isn't the original nature God gave to humanity—it is a secondary nature. The fact that sin will destroy your life proves that we weren't made to handle sin. Sin will make you uncomfortable, and it will make you feel guilty, because it's not like your primary nature. There's not one part of us that can cope with sin: not our spirits, not our minds, not our emotions, and not our bodies. Sin may bring pleasure for a little while, but in the end it will destroy. (See, for example, Hebrews 11:25; Psalm 94:23.) Romans 6:23 makes it clear that *"the wages of sin is death."* God made us for life and love. Love does not destroy; it builds and heals. Love sustains and protects us.

Paul so ably described the warfare of the two natures within us when he wrote the passage in Romans 7:19–25. Who would know better both the nature of hate and the nature of love? Paul had been a murderer, but he became one of the greatest missionaries of love the world has ever known. Read what he wrote:

> *For the good that I will to do, I do not do; but the evil I will not to do, that I practice. Now if I do what I will not to do, it is no longer I who do it, but sin that dwells in me. I find then a law, that evil is present with me, the one who wills to do good. For I delight in the law of God according to the inward man. But I see another law in my members, warring against the law of my mind, and bringing me into captivity to the law of sin which is in my members.* (Romans 7:19–23)

Paul cried out to know how he could be delivered from the warfare in his soul: *"O wretched man that I am! Who will deliver me from this body of death?"* (verse 24). But Paul had found the answer to his own question, and he answered it for you and for me when he said, *"I thank God through Jesus Christ our Lord. So then with the mind I myself serve the law of God, but with the flesh the law of sin"* (verse 25). Paul knew by experience that the power of sin is broken and the guilt and condemnation of sin is removed from those who walk according to the Spirit and not according to the flesh. (See Romans 8:1.)

When you receive Jesus, your spirit, which was dead because of sin, is renewed—and your *"new man"* lines up with the nature of God; it has the power in Christ to subdue the secondary nature.

> *...as the truth is in Jesus: that you put off, concerning your former conduct, the old man which grows corrupt according to the deceitful lusts, and be renewed in the spirit of your mind, and that you put on the new man which was created according to God, in true righteousness and holiness.*
>
> (Ephesians 4:21–23)

There is a law that comes into you and me when we are reborn that sets us free from the secondary nature. That *"law of the Spirit of life in Christ Jesus"* will set you free from sin and death because you have Christ in you, and you have been renewed by His Holy Spirit. (See Romans 8:2.) Christ in you is your hope of living in accordance with your original, primary

Christ in you is your hope of walking in all of God's goodness and glory.

nature, your expectation of walking in all of God's goodness and glory. (See Colossians 1:27.) In Christ, we can lay hold of the hope that is a sure and steadfast anchor of the soul, according to Hebrews 6:18–19. Jesus Christ, our Hope, will take us into the very presence of God.

> *For when we were in the flesh, the sinful passions which were aroused by the law were at work in our members to bear fruit to death. But now we have been delivered from the law, having died to what we were held by, so that we should serve in the newness of the Spirit and not in the oldness of the letter.* (Romans 7:5–6)

We all know that we become like those with whom we associate, so let's all take advantage of associating with Father God and His Son, Jesus Christ. Read the words of John:

> *Truly our fellowship is with the Father and with His Son Jesus Christ....Behold what manner of love the Father has bestowed on us, that we should be called children of God! Therefore the world does not know us, because it did not know Him. Beloved, **now we are children of God**; and it has not yet been revealed what we shall be, but we know that when He is revealed, we shall be like Him, for we shall see Him as He is. And **everyone who has this hope in Him purifies himself, just as He is pure**.* (1 John 1:3; 3:1–3)

The apostle John wrote more about God's love and the operation of His love in us than any other writer of the Scriptures. John was called the "beloved" apostle; he was a man who flowed in God's love because he knew and understood the love of God. However, John had not always been such a man. Before John yielded totally to God's love, he apparently often expressed his secondary nature. Jesus named John and his brother James *"the sons of thunder"* (see Mark 3:17), and one time John and James wanted Jesus to call fire down on some people. The Lord told them, in effect, that they weren't aware of the spirit (nature) from which that wrong attitude came. (See Luke 9:54–56.) However, love transformed John and James, and with the insight of the Holy Spirit, John later wrote, *"We love Him because He first loved us"* (1 John 4:19).

You didn't love God first; He loved you first. You may think you were looking for God, but all the time, He was pursuing you and watching over you, because His desire was to pour out His love upon you. You responded to His love and began to love Him back. Without receiving His kind of love, you never could have truly loved Him. Religions teach you to climb to God by doing good deeds, afflicting the body, or abiding by their rules and regulations; but no one can climb to God through his or her own efforts. Instead, Jesus is *the* Ladder that God sent down to us—His Ladder of love.

Even many Christian groups put so much stress on "doing" that their members work and work to please God. They count the Bible chapters they read, the hours they pray, and the meetings they attend. They fast and deny the flesh—always hoping to do enough to stay in God's "good graces," but never finding the liberty of God's grace that sets us free from works. What is that grace like? Because His love has touched us, we love to fellowship with Him in the Word and prayer, to fellowship with other believers, and to walk in the Spirit—*we love God.* There is such exhilarating freedom in His love!

> *There is such exhilarating freedom in God's love!*

The opportunity to speak at a Mormon women's retreat was one of the most unusual I've ever had. One woman in the group had been born again and had spearheaded the invitation. After a few sessions, some of the women challenged me for talking as though an individual could know he or she was saved. According to their doctrine, that information will be available only when Jesus comes, because salvation is dependent upon works; the greater your works, the higher your heaven. These precious, sincere women were all trying to climb to heaven on a ladder of works. It's just the opposite! We don't go up the ladder; God comes down the Ladder to the lowest rung where we are, stretches out His arms, and says, "I love you exactly as you are."

Hang on to your hats. I have a marvelous praise report from that retreat! I was told that at no time could I give an invitation to receive salvation, but God gave me different instructions. Before the last meeting, the Lord said, *I want you to go in there and offer salvation to those women.* I reminded the Lord about what I had been told, but He didn't change His mind. He reminded *me* that it was the last meeting, so what could they do? I was packing up and leaving town anyway. Aha—I found that God is smarter than I am. So, I went into that last session and presented the plan of salvation, and the hand of every woman in the room went up to receive Jesus. That is, every hand but one. That hand belonged to the born-again woman who had invited me.

Four Basic Aspects of God's Love

The Greek word *agape* is the word used for the God kind of love. The Spirit-inspired writers of the New Testament used the word in a totally different way than it had ever been used before. The noun *agape*, together with the verb *agapao*, give us

the characteristic word of Christianity,... since the Spirit of revelation has used it to express ideas previously unknown....

In respect of *agapao* as used of God, it expresses the deep and constant "love" and interest of a perfect Being towards entirely unworthy objects, producing and fostering a reverential "love" in them towards the Giver, and a practical "love" towards those who are partakers of the same, and a desire to help others to seek the Giver.[1]

---

[1] Hogg and Vine, *Notes on Thessalonians*, 105, quoted in *Vine's Complete Expository Dictionary of Old and New Testament Words* (New York: Thomas Nelson Publishers, 1985), 381–82.

Romans 5:8 says, *"But God demonstrates His own love [agape] toward us, in that while we were still sinners, Christ died for us."* God loves us and sent His Son to save us, even though we didn't deserve it. When you receive Jesus and experience agape love, that same agape love resides in you because you are one with Him. Romans 5:5 says, *"The love of God has been poured out in our hearts by the Holy Spirit who was given to us."* The love from God that fills your heart is no different from His agape love. Therefore, you have the potential to love exactly the way God loves.

> *You have the potential to love exactly the way God loves.*

I'm now going to describe four basic aspects of agape love.

1. Spontaneous and Unconditional

First, agape love is spontaneous and unconditional. God doesn't look down from His heavenly throne and pick out a good prospect to love. He isn't looking for high IQ, great physique, outstanding ability, charming personality, and so forth. No, every one of us is loved *spontaneously* by God. He doesn't wait to see if we are going to turn out good or bad, tall or short, rich or poor. God never looks for our potential before He will love us. There are simply no preconditions we have to meet in order to be loved by God. Yet we do need to respond to Him to enter into the abundant life He offers. All we have to do is step through the door into His love; the door is marked "Jesus."

2. Seeks to Give, Not to Get

The second marvelous thing about God's love is that it seeks to give, and it is indifferent to value received. After all, what of value could we possibly give to God in return for His love? He certainly deserves our love and praise, but there is isn't anything that He lacks. He is omnipotent and omniscient. We tend to like people who can give us something. They may be able to help us, promote us, get us into the right places, or do a wonderful thing for us. So, we love them for what we can get out of the deal. These people we choose have something to give us in return for our love. That isn't the way God loves. I imagine God thinking, *I may not receive love in return, but I will love anyway; I can't help loving, because I am love.* He loves the righteous as well as the unrighteous, and He *"sends rain on the just and the unjust"* (Matthew 5:45). Why? Because His nature is love, and agape love always seeks to give, not to get.

I once read about a woman whose life was spared because of agape love. It involved another incident with a burglar. One night, this lady walked into her London apartment and discovered a robber helping himself to her valuables. Right then, the man could have killed her. Who knows the fear that might have gripped her heart? However, instead of fear, there was something much better in her heart; it was the agape love of God that expects nothing in return. Instead of screaming, the lady said, "You have broken into my apartment, and you are taking the most precious things I have; evidently, you must need them more than I do, so you may have them. I give them to you, so you don't have to steal them." Then, the woman led the robber to where she had other valuables hidden and showed them to him. This totally unnerved the thief, who said, "Lady, I can't handle this," and he turned and walked out, leaving everything behind, including his gun.

3. Creative

Perhaps the most inspiring and awesome thing about God's love is that it is creative. It doesn't look for something of value, but *it takes nothing and creates something of great value.* Isn't that wonderful? We might look at somebody and see nothing worthwhile; but with a look of love, God sees a vessel of infinite value. Then, He begins His creative work.

Once time, I called a pastor whom I didn't know concerning a missions project. We chatted awhile, and he told me he had been a youth pastor in a church where I had held a Bible Encounter. Then, I remembered this pastor's testimony.

When he was seventeen years old, he and a friend got high on drugs, murdered a woman, and cut her up with a butcher knife. I know that's horrible, but just wait. The young man went to prison, and his mother and father went every weekend to see him. The mother, who was a Christian, prayed continually for her son who was unsaved, who was a murderer, and whose life was in shambles. Then, a Christian music group came to the prison, and this murderer was saved. A few weeks later, he was filled with the Holy Spirit. He was so changed by the love of God that he soon became the prison chaplain.

Seven years later, this man was among seven murderers chosen by the state attorney to be released because of their model behavior. Well, that was unheard of! His parents worried about what freedom would do to him, but after he went home, he enrolled in Bible school. After graduation, he became the youth pastor in the church where he had seen me. Later, he married a fine Christian girl and took the pastorate where he is now. The story just gets better and better. Because he had been on drugs for several years, he supposed he couldn't father any children, yet his wife presented him with triplets! Just see what God's creative love can do. As the saying goes, "God doesn't make junk." He sees everyone as a diamond in the rough. Only the touch of the Master is needed to create a sparkling gem of exquisite beauty.

4. Initiates Fellowship with God

Last, God's love initiates fellowship with Him. We were lost and undone in this world, without hope and estranged from God, until His love touched us and brought us into His family. (See Ephesians 2:12–13.) Now we can have continual fellowship with the Father and our elder brother Jesus Christ. (See Ephesians 2:12–13, 19.) You love to be around those who love you, don't you? You just feel so comfortable with them and enjoy their fellowship. The love God has for us causes us to desire His fellowship, too. I delight in God's presence and in His fellowship. I know He is my friend.

He chose us in Him before the foundation of the world, that we should be holy and without blame before Him in love, having predestined us to adoption as sons by Jesus Christ to Himself, according to the good pleasure of His will, to the praise of the glory of His grace, by which He has made us accepted in the Beloved. (Ephesians 1:4–6)

I don't enjoy being around a person who never compliments me, who never has a good word for me, a person who is always picking at me or criticizing the way I do things. You don't either. There is no real fellowship with a person like that. However, when we have full assurance of someone's love, we can receive constructive criticism and feel built up rather than torn down. It's the same with God. Even when He corrects us, it's so sweet because we know it comes out of His love. God's loving correction keeps us on course and prevents us from making mistakes. We would miss all that if we weren't in fellowship with a God who loves us and cares about what happens to us. First John 1:7 says that when we walk in the light as God is in the light, we have fellowship with Him and with one another.

Love Yourself and Others with God's Love

Does God expect us to love ourselves? We are able to give love back to God because He planted His love in our hearts, but what about loving ourselves? That is often the hardest thing in the world to do, but the Lord tells us to love others *as we love ourselves.* (See Matthew 19:19.) I have counted nine times in the New Testament where the love we are commanded to have for others is based on the love we have for ourselves. Many people are harder on themselves than they are on anyone else. If you go around hating or disliking yourself, in spite of God's love for you, you're out of the will of God. Are you going to love what God loves and hate what God hates? Well, God loves you, so love yourself.

Since we have the agape love of God in us that enables us to love Him, we can also love ourselves with agape love. That doesn't mean that you will always be pleased with yourself or that you should ignore the mistakes you make because you are so extra special to you. Nor does it mean that you can run roughshod over other people. That is selfishness, not love. Let's look again at the four attributes of God's love, and then we will learn how we can properly and constructively love ourselves.

First, your love must be unconditional. You can't love yourself when you are "good" and then hate yourself when you are "bad." Love for self is not based on achievement or the value others place on you. You must love yourself even when you waste an entire day, or when you stick your foot in your mouth and embarrass everyone, including yourself. Loving yourself with God's love creates something in you that gives you a good self-image. You see, God loves you exactly as you are right now. He sees every fault and every asset, but none of these things alters His love for you in any way.

God's love brings immeasurable security to our lives. It enables us to be secure about ourselves. This kind of security enables you to correct your mistakes

> *The way to satisfaction, success, and creative fulfillment is to place the same value on your life that God does.*

without self-condemnation and to regard your achievements without pride. When you "blow it," repent and always remember you're in the making for something better. *"For it is God who works in you both to will and to do for His good pleasure"* (Philippians 2:13). The way to satisfaction, success, and creative fulfillment is to place the same value on your life that God does. Proper appreciation of self will cause you to enjoy your own company—even *others* will enjoy your company—but your best fellowship will be with the Lord. Agape love of self brings contentment to the heart, rewarding friendships with others, and satisfying, refreshing fellowship with God.

Now that you love yourself, you can love anyone else as God loves him or her. Does that sound like an impossible assignment? Not when you love others with agape love. The love of God with which you love Him and love yourself is the same love with which you can love others. God's love resides within you, and it doesn't take a vacation when you encounter someone you "just can't stand." Remember, agape love is unconditional. It isn't enough just to love your friends; you must love your enemies. That's agape. Jesus said that even the heathen can love their own friends, but the mark of a believer is found in the love he has for his enemies. Ouch! (See, for example, Matthew 5:43–48.)

It's easy to love people who dress as we dress, enjoy the same kind of movies we enjoy, like the same restaurants we like, share the same opinions, and have similar backgrounds or education. We relate to these kinds of people, don't we? However, God's love in us will love spontaneously and will have no self-serving motivation. Allow yourself to see others through the Lord's eyes, and you will "fall in love" with people. When you love as God loves, you will be indifferent to value; your love will not be determined by whether or not an individual can be of value to you. How freeing it is to find something you can do for others instead of looking for something they can do for you. You will never come out on the short end. God will repay all your kindness and love.

It is so exciting to know that I can create something worthwhile in other people just by loving and encouraging them. A young man who became an employee of our church had previously attended our Christian school and played basketball on the school team. He told my husband, Wally, this story, which brought a smile to my face: Every time he was up for a free throw, I would yell at the top of my lungs, "Come on, you can do it; you're good, you're good!" He didn't think he was really good, but he thought, *I'd better be good, because Marilyn is expecting me to be good.* You know what? He would always do better than he thought he could. How important is a free throw? Well, how important is it to build confidence in an individual? The young man never forgot that, and I believe he became a better achiever because I encouraged him to be one.

> *God's love for others builds bridges over which we can walk into wonderful fellowship.*

God's love for others builds bridges over which we can walk into wonderful fellowship. When you love with God's love, it's easy to have fellowship. In a real relationship, you don't major on differences, even though there will always be differences; no two individuals are alike. In true fellowship, people always find something to enjoy about one another; they enjoy conversation or simply the presence of that other individual. Did you ever meet someone you didn't know, but when the two of you discovered you were both Christians, there was immediate fellowship? There was instant communication as the love of God flowed between you.

I have a great example from a lady who called our prayer line to share a wonderful praise report. This lady frequently walked to a park near her home and enjoyed sitting there on a bench. She and another woman, who were only "park bench acquaintances," started visiting with one another. One day, the lady disclosed to her "friend" that a large growth had been found in her abdomen. Immediately, the other woman prayed for her, and God performed a miracle. The lady felt pain and movement in her abdomen, and after examination she could no longer feel the growth. It had disappeared! Why did the lady call *our* prayer line with this good report? Because the woman who prayed for her attended our church. Praise the Lord, we are "creating" agape lovers!

A Major Theme in God's Word

We've looked at four aspects of agape love, and there are also four things that love *does*: it forgives, it covers sin, it heals, and it creates. I want to examine the lives of three people who made love their major theme when they wrote portions of the Word of God. One of these people is Peter, who began his walk with Jesus as a headstrong, uneducated fisherman. Nevertheless, Jesus hung in with him because He loved Peter with unconditional love. The devil tried to "sift Peter like wheat," but Jesus prayed for him. (See Luke 22:31–32.) Peter's denial of Christ seemed evidence enough that he didn't really love Jesus, but Jesus came to Peter with His love and asked, "Peter, do you love Me?" Peter realized he couldn't love Jesus with his own love; he ran out of it. (See John 21:15–19.) Only God's love, which was poured out into Peter's heart by the Holy Spirit, could stand the test. (See Romans 5:5.) Peter learned to draw on that love, and in 1 Peter 4:8, he wrote that love covers a multitude of sins. Peter had learned this truth by experience.

Love created a new man out of Peter, and then Peter "created" another new man with that same love. It was a young man named John Mark. After Paul refused to take John Mark on his next missionary journey, Peter took him under his wing. John Mark had been with Paul on a missions trip to Pamphylia, but the young man had quit and "gone home to Mama." At the time, that was enough for Paul, but Peter worked with John Mark and made him his spiritual son. This loving encouragement created a man whom the Holy Spirit could use to write the gospel of Mark. Although Mark was not one of the disciples who had walked with Jesus, Peter imparted to him all the information necessary to write the gospel. Can't you just see Mark listening with rapt attention as the older man lovingly shared his experiences with the Lord? And, after a while, Paul and Mark were reconciled; Paul wrote to Timothy, *"Get Mark and bring him with you, for he is useful to me for ministry"* (2 Timothy 4:11).

Now, let's take a look at John. Everybody thinks "the beloved apostle" was so sweet, but he wasn't sweet when he started. Remember how I told you that Jesus called him a "son of thunder" because of his temper, and that, one time, John and his brother James even wanted to destroy some Samaritans with fire? And their mother was brash enough to ask Jesus if they could sit in major places of authority on either side of Christ when He came into His kingdom. John was apparently the kind who would have shoved people out of line at the supermarket. What transformed this man? It was the love with which Jesus loved him. You can't rub elbows with love without that love rubbing off on you.

> *You can't rub elbows with love without that love rubbing off on you.*

This same man later went to the Samaritans, whom he had wanted to burn up, and he and Peter prayed with them to receive the baptism with the Holy Spirit. (See Acts 8:14–17.) Love changed a man who had murder in his heart into a man who just wanted to share and minister the love of God. Jesus created agape love in John's heart, and John turned around and created that same love in others. While Jesus was on earth, John loved Him so much that he always stayed close to Him. He gained an unusual understanding of God's love, and he wrote more clearly about love in one gospel and three small epistles than most any other writer of Scripture. Today, God's love is still creating and changing the lives of those who take John's writings to heart.

The third man who was dramatically changed by the creative power of God's love is Paul. It was Paul who held the coats of those who stoned Stephen for his faith in Jesus, giving assent to his murder. That's not all! Paul was such a zealous Jew that he traveled hundreds of miles, even across national boundaries, to arrest members of the heretical "sect" of Christians. Then, these Christians were often murdered for their faith. Today, we might describe Paul as a mass murderer, and yet Jesus loved this hateful man so much that He personally appeared to Paul after His resurrection and ascension and turned him around in the direction of love. The encounter with God's love healed Paul's heart and created a totally new man. (See Acts 7:57–8:4; 9:1–22; 26:9–20.)

Talk about a changed heart! Paul said he loved his fellow Jews so much that, if it were possible, he would give up his own salvation to win their salvation. (See Romans 9:1–5.) If that isn't the God kind of love, I don't know what is. Who would give up his own salvation and give it to another? Paul expressed a willingness to spend eternity in hell for the sake of men who were trying to murder him. First

Corinthians 13, the Love Chapter of the Bible, was written by Paul. What a revelation it is of God's love for us, as well as His love working through us. No one knew better than Paul the creative miracle of God's love.

Surrendering to God's Love Will Conquer Fear

If we are going to walk in the fullness of God's love, then we need to know what can hinder that love from working in our lives. First John 4:18 says, *"There is no fear in love; but perfect love casts out fear, because fear involves torment. But he who fears has not been made perfect in love."*

What keeps us from being loving? What keeps our hearts all upset? A major reason is *fear!* Fear comes, bringing torment with it, when we are not secure in God's love. If we are not really sure God loves us, or if we think we aren't good enough for Him to love, then we open ourselves to fear. Have you heard the warning against "taking your life into your own hands"? That is exactly what we do when we allow insecurity and fear to cause us to doubt God's ability to profitably guide our lives. When we take our lives into our own hands, we will make all kinds of mistakes that reinforce our fears.

We can also develop fear in regard to situations and other people. This fear is filled with dread and devoid of faith. Fear comes into your life when you look at your circumstances instead of at Jesus. Fear of circumstances will torment your soul and your body. The spirit of fear will move in all areas of your life, hindering and hurting you. Once you give in to your fears, they will grow until they become bondages. Fear can make you unstable in your thinking. When you let it go for too long, it becomes a phobia that will envelop your mind and hold you tight in paranoia.

How do we get rid of fear? Jesus is once again our best example. In John 12:27, about a week before His arrest and crucifixion, Jesus said, *"Now My soul is troubled, and what shall I say? 'Father, save Me from this hour'? But for this purpose I came to this hour."* What caused Jesus to be troubled? Certain Greeks had come to worship at Jerusalem, and they asked to see Jesus. When Andrew and Philip conveyed this message, the Lord said, *"The hour has come that the Son of Man should be glorified"* (verse 23). Then, He told them He was destined to die. I believe the Greeks would have changed that destiny by taking Jesus to Greece and making Him a great philosopher in a culture that held wisdom and learning in the highest esteem. The Jews persecuting Him were already looking for a reason to crucify Him, and Jesus was being tempted to leave Jerusalem.

We know that as a man, Jesus shrank from the cross; it was a fearful thing to face. In Gethsemane, Jesus was so troubled that *"His sweat became like great drops of blood falling down to the ground"* (Luke 22:44). What caused Jesus to fear? It was the cross. Jesus struggled in great agony when faced with the cross. He knew He could walk away from it all—and leave you and me behind. However, Jesus conquered the fear that tried to grip Him and *surrendered* to the Father's will. He said, *"Not My will, but Yours, be done"* (Luke 22:42). How was Jesus able to face the cross? He surrendered to the Father because He knew the Father's will was best. Again, on the cross, Jesus was troubled and fearful when He cried, *"My God, My God, why have You forsaken Me?"* (Matthew 27:46). However, Jesus' last utterance from the cross was one of surrender when He released His spirit into His Father's hands. (See Luke 23:46.)

Another example for us in regard to fear is Paul. Paul was so surrendered to the will of God that he could write from a Roman jail,

> *But I want you to know, brethren, that the things which happened to me have actually turned out for the furtherance of the gospel, so that it has become evident to the whole palace guard, and to all the rest, that my chains are in Christ; and most of the brethren in the Lord, having become confident by my chains, are much more bold to speak the word without fear.*   (Philippians 1:12–14)

Paul wasn't afraid of being in prison because it caused other Christians to lose their fear and to preach boldly the Word of God. In prison, Paul was able to win members of Caesar's household to Christ. (See Philippians 4:22.) Of course, we know it was while Paul was imprisoned that he wrote six of his thirteen epistles, which comprise a major portion of the New Testament. He wasn't out preaching the gospel, but those letters have reached millions of people.

Paul was no stranger to the inside of a jail, but it didn't disturb his peace. Once, when he was beaten and thrown into jail, Paul was still singing praises to the Lord at midnight. This man wasn't whining and pining, because he knew God would work out everything for his good. God was so pleased that He opened the prison doors with an earthquake; but Paul didn't leave. Instead, he stayed and led the jailer to Jesus. The jailer got his family, and the whole bunch were saved. (See Acts 16:23–34.) Paul never looked for comfort; he looked for results. Men could throw Paul into prison, but they couldn't throw him into fear, because he was secure in God's love. It was Paul who wrote these words in Romans 8:28: *"And we know that all things work together for good to those who love God, to those who are the called according to His purpose."*

God will release you from your fear. Fix your heart on His Word. The Word of God will stabilize your emotions and put your focus on Him. The more you have the Word and the more you hold on to it, the more established you are in God's promises and blessings. Believe that God can take all things and work them together for good. When you are afraid, be honest with the Lord. Tell Him that you are afraid, that

The Word of God will stabilize your emotions and put your focus on Him.

you don't like it, that you feel it's the opposite of faith, that you're sorry for it, and that you repent of it. Say, "Lord, I'm going to trust You to take care of me in this matter." Saturate yourself in God's love. He cares for you and wants to take away your fears. *"For God has not given us a spirit of fear, but of power and of love and of a sound mind"* (2 Timothy 1:7). And He will deliver you. (See Psalm 34:4.) Psalm 56:3 says, *"Whenever I am afraid, I will trust in You."*

What did Jesus do in fearful circumstances? What did Paul do? They surrendered to God! I believe any areas of our lives that are not surrendered to the Lord will keep us in fear. You may not always realize your fears, but do you believe God loves you? Do you think He is big enough to take care of you? If you do, you can totally surrender to the Lord, and all fear, known and unknown, will then be in His hands. When you are surrendered to God, He is able to take care of any trial you face, no matter how big it looks to you. Maybe all you can do is be willing to surrender. God will accept that and strengthen your will. Do you realize to what you are surrendering? You are surrendering to God's love. Remember John's words: *"There is no fear in love; but perfect love casts out fear"* (1 John 4:18).

Surrendering to God's Love Will Conquer Bitterness

Another thing that keeps us from walking in the fullness of God's love is bitterness and resentment toward others. When I eat something bitter, my mouth contracts as if it's in pain, and my teeth are set on edge. A bitter attitude, such as anger or discontentment, sets your physical body on edge. You can become bitter if you don't forgive and forget the hurts that are heaped on you by your spouse, children, parents, employer, neighbors, or government. You may feel you have a right to be bitter because of your pain, but that bitterness will hurt you more than the other people's actions did.

The root of bitterness grows a variety of fruit, including hatefulness, self-loathing, despair, strife, jealousy, and confusion. That bitter fruit is shared with others, and when they taste it, they can become bitter, too. When you spread your bitterness to others, *you* will be defiled. I believe bitterness hinders your faith. When you harbor a wounded attitude, you aren't trusting God to take care of you, heal you, and avenge you. And lack of faith can keep God from hearing your prayers.

Unforgiveness can affect your thinking, strength, anointing, health, and the direction of your life. When you harbor unforgiveness in your heart, you give place to the devil to wreak havoc in your life and your physical body. Unforgiveness brings death to your life by causing you to focus on the person who committeed the offense. In contrast, forgiveness paralyzes the hand of the devil. It takes the sting out of the offense and causes you to focus on Jesus. It releases you and the person who has offended you from the offense, and it frees God to bring about a change in both of you.

When you feel bitter, examine the reason you feel the way you do and get rid of it by laying it at Jesus' feet. If you don't allow grief to follow its natural course (you must allow yourself to feel the pain, and you must take it to the Lord), then you will become angry and discontent. Turn to God so that He can move in the situation and heal your attitude. If you repent, God will forgive and cleanse you. (See Psalm 55:15; 1 John 1:9.) When Jesus died on the cross, He drank the bitter cup of our sins; our bitterness will be cleansed by the blood of Jesus.

If you don't repent of the sin of bitterness, you will keep it, and it will grow. You must forgive the person who offended you. Here are four steps to forgiving:

- Understand that the devil is responsible for the offense.

- Separate the person from the sin. Hate the sin, not the person. Get angry at the devil.

- Make the decision NOW to forgive everyone who has ever offended you.

- Bless those who have offended you, according to Luke 6:27–28: *"But I say to you who hear: Love your enemies, do good to those who hate you, bless those who curse you, and pray for those who spitefully use you."*

Surrendering to God's Love Will Conquer Depression

Third, surrendering to God's love will conquer depression. Depression causes you to feel burdened, gloomy, and sad. It is therefore an open door to the devil's attacks. Self-pity causes you to take your eyes off the supernatural. You yield to self-pity when you begin to think and talk about the problem. This sets the stage for the devil to steal your joy.

The root of most depression is disobedience and rebellion against God. Bad circumstances in our lives can also cause depression. You can fight sadness and depression with the joy of the Lord. Cast your depression on Him and begin to worship Him. Sing *"psalms and hymns and spiritual songs, singing and making melody in your heart to the Lord"* (Ephesians 5:19). Make a decision to rejoice in every situation instead of waiting for the circumstances to dictate how you feel. Don't allow your circumstances to determine your spiritual state. Take control of the situation with praise and worship.

> *Don't allow your circumstances to determine your spiritual state. Take control of the situation with praise and worship.*

"The joy of the LORD is your strength" (Nehemiah 8:10). Rejoicing in the Lord elevates you above the situation and enables you to enter into a childlike faith. *"Rejoice in the Lord always. Again I will say, rejoice!"* (Philippians 4:4). Continue to rejoice in the Lord until you see a breakthough in your situation. Rejoicing communicates to the devil that you have already won. (See 1 Corinthians 15:57.)

Remember that joy and laughter are good medicine and can make you well. Genuine, heartfelt laughter affects your attitude, your health, and the way you are received by others. *"A merry heart does good, like medicine, but a broken spirit dries the bones"* (Proverbs 17:22).

"Heart Checkups"

Wrong attitudes are harmful because they can defeat you spiritually. Attitudes that cause anxiety and depression are often related to family problems, unhappy work situations, and wrong thoughts toward yourself and others. Good attitudes are like medicine to your bones and health to all your flesh. (See Proverbs 4:20–22.) You need regular "heart checkups," so that the Holy Spirit can check for bitterness, fearfulness, depression, or hatefulness. *"Search me, O God, and know my heart; try me, and know my anxieties; and see if there is any wicked way in me, and lead me in the way everlasting"* (Psalm 139:23–24). Here is how to have a "heart checkup":

- Ask God to tell you if there is any wicked way in you.

- When you listen for the truth about your heart, He can deal with you effectively.

- Repent of your negative emotions.

- God will strengthen your soul and give you a steadfast heart so you can be victorious in your circumstances. (See Psalm 138:3.)

Keep a right attitude in the various changes in your life, hold on to God, and say what the Word says; then, you'll come through very well. Spend time in the Word and in prayer, and keep your faith and confidence in God.

Habits are created through a process that begins with a single thought. Dwelling on certain thoughts can lead to actions. Through habits, you reap a lifestyle, and that lifestyle will bring either death or abundant life. This is why we need to allow God and His love to guide our spirits. He will control our minds and emotions and give us life more abundantly. (See Romans 8:6 NIV.)

If you know Jesus, His perfect love is in your heart. It's God's supernatural agape love that heals the broken heart. Jesus is your heart mender!

Life Under the Son

Do you like popcorn? Yes or no, you will just love the kind of popcorn I'm going to serve you now! This popcorn is far better than Cracker Jack or cheese corn; it's "testimony" corn. I'm just going to serve you some "popcorn" testimonies of a few dynamic and wonderful healings that have taken place in our Bible Encounters. One of the most unusual miracles of healing took place not long after the Lord began to confirm the Word, which I was teaching, with signs following:

> *And they went forth, and preached every where, the Lord working with them, and confirming the word with signs following.*
> (Mark 16:20 KJV)

One evening during a service, I was just praying a general prayer for healing. I didn't ask people to stand, nor were hands laid on anyone, but God moved. After the prayer, a woman and her daughter testified that both of them had a "necklace" of small warts instantly removed from around their necks. It was an inherited problem that afflicted other women in the family, also. You see, God is so loving that even the "smallest" things are not overlooked by Him. Don't ever think your problem is too small for our great big God.

A more dramatic healing occurred when a small child who had never heard a sound received her hearing. This little girl wasn't even in the service, but her mother was anointed with oil in proxy for the child, who was in the church nursery. This precious mother had come with faith in her heart for her two-year-old. A while later, everyone's attention was drawn to the rear of the auditorium when a *very* excited woman rushed through the door. It was the mother of the deaf child. After prayer, she had slipped out and gone to the nursery to check her little girl. She'd been overwhelmed with joy when she'd found that God had opened both the child's ears. The pastor of the church knew the woman and her child, so he verified the healing. A wave of praise and thanksgiving swept through the congregation when the child was brought to the front and we proved she could hear perfectly!

Here's another testimony concerning a six-year-old boy who was having as many as six severe nosebleeds a day. After prayer, the boy was healed of this terrible hemorrhaging, which was draining away his very life. Nothing had been able to stop it—but God did! A year later, his mother reported that her son had not had one nosebleed since we'd prayed. I also remember a woman who had two lumps in her breast, one on her arm, and two on her neck. After prayer, they disappeared—lumps, bumps, and all!

In another service, a woman's knee was healed. After three surgeries, the knee was still popping and giving the lady extreme pain. Her knee was healed during the anointing service, and the delighted lady began to run up and down the aisles. Now, that's a good "popcorn" testimony, isn't it? It's much better than popping knees! Has my special bowl of popcorn strengthened your faith for healing? That is exactly what I want it to do. The same healing power of God that touched these people is able to touch you and those you love.

> *The healing power of God is able to touch you and those you love.*

Life Under the Sun or Life Under the Son

Everyone under the sun is subject to all kinds of afflictions and ailments, but all these things have to melt away when we live in the light of the S-o-n. That is God's Son, the Lord Jesus Christ! I want to show you some exciting truth from a very philosophical book in the Bible, the book of Ecclesiastes. I used to have trouble enjoying this portion of the Scriptures because it seemed to be just a book of moans and groans. In fact, I called it the "book of old groans." The writer was always saying everything was "vanity." I thought the message was hopeless and depressing—until the Holy Spirit revealed to me what was really being said there. Wow, what an exciting book it became!

Solomon, the author of Ecclesiastes, kept using the phrase *"under the sun"* throughout the book; but I want you to compare with me life under the sun to life under the Son. What a difference! It took a long time for the wisest man who ever lived to get back to this truth after he had left the light of God's wisdom and satisfaction to seek the wisdom and pleasure of the world. And what did Solomon find in life under the sun? Trying to prove to himself that the world's way was better, this "wisest" of all men found only *vanity*. His search had been all in vain. As James wrote,

> *Who among you is wise or clever? Let his right conduct give practical proof of it, with the modesty that comes of wisdom. But if you are harboring bitter jealousy and **selfish ambition** in your hearts, consider whether your claims are not false, and a defiance of the truth. This is not the wisdom that comes from above, it is earthbound, sensual, demonic....But the wisdom from above is in the first place pure, and then peace-loving, considerate, and open to reason; it is straightforward and sincere, rich in mercy and in the kindly deeds that are its fruit.* (James 3:13–17 NEB)

King Solomon was no different from the rest of us. What can we expect when we live *under* the circumstances of life? If you listen to all the advertisements on TV and read what is in the newspaper, you can expect to feel bad or to be overtaken by some sort of evil. Most all of the products advertised are to make you well because you are sick, make you clean because you are dirty, make you smell good because you stink—or satisfy every lustful desire of your flesh. That is *life under the sun*. Solomon advised us to remember the Creator while we are young, before the evil days come and the years draw near when we find no pleasure in life. (See Ecclesiastes 12:1.)

What was Solomon saying? He was saying we had better remember God while we are young, because when we get older, our bodies will wear out, and our minds will be clouded, so that we won't be able to enjoy God or life anymore. Solomon then painted a word picture of what is going to happen to an aging body. In allegorical fashion, he described feet as *"keepers of the house,"* knees as *"strong men,"* teeth as *"grinders,"* and eyes and ears as *"windows"* and *"doors."* (See verses 3–4.) Solomon said old feet are going to tremble and old knees are going to bow, so that a person can no longer stand or walk without difficulty. In other words, the body will become feeble. Solomon said the aged are going to lose their teeth and experience dim eyesight and loss of hearing. Fear will be exaggerated because the body won't be physically able to handle what it could in younger days.

All this is Solomon's morbid, yet accurate, description of the aging process of the human body. He even mentioned the graying of hair when he said that the "almond tree will blossom." (See verse 5.) Solomon went on with this dismal and discouraging discourse by saying it is a burden for the aged to pick up a grasshopper, meaning that work becomes burdensome and an almost impossible task. Even the desire for food will fail. At *this* point, there's virtually nothing left to bring excitement or pleasure to life. Solomon concluded by saying there is nothing in the future for someone in this condition except to go to the *"long home"* (verse 5), which is his way of describing death. Only the mourners remain to remind anyone of the dead. With an outlook like that, no wonder Solomon said, *"Vanity of vanities, all is vanity"* (Ecclesiastes 1:2).

Solomon then made some interesting observations about what happened when someone died in his day. Ecclesiastes 12:6 says, *"Remember your Creator before the silver cord is loosed, or the golden bowl is broken, or the pitcher shattered at the fountain, or the wheel broken at the well."*

At that time in the Middle East, a bridegroom didn't always give his bride a ring. Instead, he would give her a silver cord to wear around her neck. When the husband died, the wife removed the silver cord and placed it on his body, and it was buried with him. When an individual died, the eldest son held over the head of the deceased a pottery bowl painted in some way with gold. This bowl was filled with fire and was broken by the son to indicate that the "broken" body, which would return to the dust, had released the spirit to ascend into the presence of God.

If the mourners touched either the body or the bier upon which the body was placed, they had to wash themselves with water. According to Jewish law, people were "unclean" if they touched a dead body or anything a dead body touched, so this washing was necessary. Afterward, they broke the special pitcher containing the cleansing water, and all the personal effects of the dead were burned. We understand now that God gave these laws to prevent the spread of disease. The *"wheel broken at the well"* refers to the bier or wagon that carried the body. Certain designated men would "put their shoulder to the wheel" and move the body to the burial place.

In those days, it was customary for everyone in town to attend a funeral. When a father died, these people became witnesses to a very important procedure. The birthright privileges were ceremonially passed on to whichever son had been designated to receive the double portion. Under normal circumstances, this was the eldest son, who was now to be the "king" (leader) and "priest" (spiritual head) of the family in the stead of his father.

This son was customarily given a brightly colored robe, such as Jacob gave Joseph, and a key was placed on his shoulders. Then, the "birthright" son would put his hands on the corpse and close the eyes of his father. All these things indicated the son's inheritance and new authority in the family. When God told Jacob to go to his son Joseph in Egypt, He said, *"Joseph will put his hand on your eyes"* (Genesis 46:4). Although Joseph was not the eldest son, the Lord confirmed with those words that Joseph was to receive the birthright and the double inheritance (even though the line of the Messiah would come through his brother Judah, as Jacob prophesied: *"The scepter shall not depart from Judah, nor a lawgiver from between his feet, until Shiloh* [the Messiah] *comes; and to Him shall be the obedience of the people"* [Genesis 49:10]).

The prophet Isaiah referred to this ceremony when he spoke prophetically of Jesus, God's birthright Son:

> *I will clothe him with your robe and strengthen him with your belt; I will commit your responsibility into his hand. He shall be a father to the inhabitants of Jerusalem and to the house of Judah. The key of the house of David I will lay on his shoulder; so he shall open, and no one shall shut; and he shall shut, and no one shall open.*
>
> (Isaiah 22:21–22)

Now that I've told you everything you didn't want to hear about death and dying, let me tell you some wonderful news. Because Jesus died—and rose again—He had the right to pass on the birthright privileges to every born-again believer. The same authority and power of Christ have been given to us as kings and priests in God's kingdom. (See Revelation 1:5–6.) Every believer has been clothed with a robe of righteousness, and Jesus Himself said,

> *And I will give you the keys of the kingdom of heaven, and whatever you bind* [lock or close] *on earth will be bound in heaven, and whatever you loose* [unlock or open] *on earth will be loosed in heaven.*
>
> (Matthew 16:19)

And to the angel of the church in Philadelphia write, "These things says He who is holy, He who is true, 'He who has the key of David, He who opens and no one shuts, and shuts and no one opens: I know your works. See, I have set before you an open door, and no one can shut it; for you have a little strength, have kept My word, and have not denied My name.'"

(Revelation 3:7–8)

Paul wrote,

For if by the one man's offense death reigned through the one, much more those who receive abundance of grace and of the gift of righteousness will reign in life through the One, Jesus Christ.   (Romans 5:17)

Oh, what good news! We don't have to live and die "under the sun." We can live under the Son and die in victory. In Luke 10:19, Jesus said, *"Behold, I give you the authority to trample on serpents and scorpions, and over all the power of the enemy, and nothing shall by any means hurt you."* Life doesn't have to be a drag that just descends to the grave; in Christ, life can be a continual celebration that ascends into the very presence of God. You won't always be happy—you will encounter grief and pain—but you can always have the joy of the Lord, which is your strength! (See Nehemiah 8:10.)

Did you know that something supernatural happened to you when you were born again that

> *The Holy Spirit, the Spirit of life, is indwelling you, and He is continually quickening your mortal body.*

absolutely changed and transformed your life? The Holy Spirit, that Spirit of life, is indwelling you. He witnesses to you that you are God's child (see Romans 8:16), and He is continually quickening your mortal body (see verse 11 KJV).

The word *"quicken"* means "to make alive." If you have God's Spirit in you, with what kind of life are you being quickened? Your physical body is being made alive with God's life. No longer do you have to be ruled and dominated by the decaying process of your natural body; your body must submit to the supernatural life of God.

There is now, *right now*, a life-giving principle working in you that will sustain your body until the end. As you grow old, you don't have to experience feeble knees, failing eyesight, loss of hearing, or a quavering voice. You don't have to be frightened at the slightest sound or exhausted with the smallest task. Life doesn't have to be that way for you under the SON, because you have the Holy Spirit quickening your mortal body! Someday, you will receive an immortal body, one that cannot die; but right now, the Spirit of life can supernaturally sustain the mortal body that is going to die:

> *But those who wait on the LORD shall renew their strength; they shall mount up with*

wings like eagles, they shall run and not be
weary, they shall walk and not faint.

(Isaiah 40:31)

This is a concept almost too hard for our minds to grasp, but let me tell you of my own personal experience. I have more energy and more strength at seventy-nine than I had in my twenties. When I was in my twenties, I was always whining and complaining about being tired.

My husband would come home and ask, "How are you?"

My stock answer was, "I'm so tired!" Because Wally got "so tired" of hearing those words, he said my theme song was, "I'm tired." He would really irritate me by singing to me an old song titled "Tired, I'm So Tired." I wanted to slap him.

To be sure, teaching school and being a homemaker kept me busy. But that schedule didn't begin to compare with my schedule today, and now I'm full of vigor and vitality!

What is the difference? In those days, I was living life *under the sun.* I did not know how to live life *under the Son*; I didn't even know that kind of life was available. When I heard about the quality of life I could have in Christ, I began to appropriate that life, and I retired "tired." Today, I'm not going downhill; I'm going uphill. And I intend to continue this upward climb until the day my body dies or Jesus takes me in the rapture. You know, Christians shouldn't just be looking for healing; we should be expecting divine health. Every Christian should stay healthy!

How to Have "Giant" Mentality

In the thirteenth chapter of Numbers, a story of faith and a story of doubt are recorded. Moses sent twelve men to spy out the land that God had promised the Israelites. This preview of Canaan was intended to encourage the people with a report of all the good things God was giving to them. However, ten of these spies came back with an "evil," fear-filled report of Canaanite giants who would surely keep Israel from the Promised Land. Ten leaders of Israel saw themselves as grasshoppers before these seemingly gigantic problems. Yet because Joshua and Caleb believed the Word of God, they saw themselves as giants and the giants as grasshoppers. Only two men had a view of faith.

Joshua and Caleb stood before the people and said,

> *The land we passed through to spy out is an exceedingly good land. If the* Lord *delights in us, then He will bring us into this land and give it to us, "a land which flows with milk and honey." Only **do not rebel** against the* Lord, ***nor fear the people** of the land, for they are our bread; their protection has departed from them, and the* Lord *is with us. Do not fear them.* (Numbers 14:7–9)

Joshua and Caleb were fearlessly able to view themselves as the giants who could devour the people of Canaan. To them, these people were going to be "the breakfast of champions." Joshua and Caleb were living life under the S-o-n! These two faith-filled men knew that it could be done; Israel could take the land flowing with milk and honey. Instead of seeing giants, Caleb and Joshua saw the good land. They even brought back some of its bounty for the others to see. However, the towering obstacles obscured the good things from the view of most of Israel and caused the majority of the people to decide that it couldn't be done. You see, they were living life under the s-u-n.

Joshua and Caleb had *giant* mentality. Because they believed they could do anything God said they could do, they lived their lives in the supernatural! Joshua and Caleb looked at what God could do instead of what they couldn't do. The unbelieving crowd had "grasshopper" mentality; because they were overcome by every problem, they continued to live life in the natural. These people were so busy looking at what they couldn't do that they could never see what God could do.

Have you ever wondered why some Christians are more successful in life than others? It all depends on one's outlook—whether a person looks at life under the sun or under the Son. Some people have "grasshopper" vision. They are so busy looking at what they aren't that they don't see what they can be and do in God. Those with "giant" vision see

Those with "giant" vision see themselves as God sees them, and they become what they want to be.

themselves as God sees them, and they become what they want to be. The first group is unsuccessful; the second group is successful. Even though you are a Christian, success comes only when you see yourself in the proper perspective and act accordingly. That's living under the Son.

This testimony from a woman who wrote to the ministry is an example of someone with "giant" vision. The lady had been suffering with cancer and had experienced severe pain in her back and in her lungs. Every day, she listened to my TV program and said with me, "This is the best day of my life, because Jesus lives big in me!" This woman envisioned herself healed and well. One day, when I prayed for the sick, this woman s-t-r-e-t-c-h-e-d out her faith into the land of promise. Within two hours, most of her pain was gone, and she was able to breathe freely. She wrote, "Eleven months ago I wasn't supposed to live overnight, but God spared me and *I am being healed.*" This precious lady sees herself well. She is living life under the Son, and she will conquer this illness.

Let's go back to the wilderness, or desert. God severely judged the Israelites' unbelief and told them they would wander in that wilderness for forty years until all the "grasshoppers" died. The unbelievers said they couldn't go into the land—and they didn't go into the land. God judged them by the words of their own mouths. There were Joshua and Caleb, stuck with a bunch of whining cowards for forty years. What were they going to do? They did exactly what Moses did; they stuck it out. Because they had a vision of promise, they were able to survive the wilderness experience. Caleb had walked all over the area of Hebron and claimed it as his own. Caleb told Moses that Hebron was the spot he wanted. He always looked forward to the day when Hebron would be his possession.

Caleb could have said, "What's the use? I'll never get Hebron. I'll wander around in this wilderness for forty years, and then I'll die here. I'm forty years old now, and by the time we spend forty more years out here and another five or six years taking the land, I'll be at least eighty-five years old—too old to enjoy anything." However, Caleb didn't think that way. Even though he would be over eighty when Israel possessed Canaan, he made a decision to live under the *Son* instead of under the *sun*. He decided that whatever time he would live in Hebron, it would still be wonderful. He settled in for the long haul and determined that no matter what came his way, he would come through. You see, Caleb and Joshua had God's promise that they would enter the land; they held tightly to that promise, and they did enter it!

When we are in church or when everything is going well, it's easy to say, "Glory to God, I'm going to live in the supernatural." Then, when tomorrow comes and the bill collector is at the door, bad news arrives, you lose your job, your kids bring home bad grades, and your mate gets angry with you, what do you do? Are you going to live in the natural, observe all the "signs of the times," and be devoured by the giants? Or, are you going to live in the supernatural, feast on God's Word, and devour your giants? Are you going to live life under the *sun* or live life under the *Son*?

Now, let's see what Caleb had to come through. This man had to conquer "giants" in the wilderness before he ever faced the giants in Canaan. How would you like to be with two million murmuring people for forty years? Are you cool, calm, and collected when your boss gets angry with you or when your kids are fussing and complaining? We all have some idea of what Caleb faced; and yet, he set his face toward Canaan. Yes, Caleb had Moses, Aaron, and Joshua who were living in the supernatural. There was a faithful minority, which also included the younger generation; but this group was greatly outnumbered at first by the majority who were walking a purely natural path.

What about the climate? I don't think it would be too wonderful to spend forty years in a desert. In order for the people to survive the climate, God provided a pillar of cloud by day to shield them from the awful heat and a pillar of fire by night to warm them when the desert became extremely cold. There were also those poisonous snakes that caused the deaths of many Israelites after they murmered and complained. (See Numbers 21:4–9.) That's not to mention the other "critters" that were probably there in the desert. God always made a provision for the people, but the desert certainly was not paradise. And Caleb had to stay there with those unbelievers when they all could have been in Canaan.

Then, there was that monotonous diet. We all enjoy variety in our meals, and these people were no exception. Food is a very important part of life. Not only is it nutritious, but it is also enjoyable. Look at most of us, and you can see how much we enjoy food. Nevertheless, anyone can "burn out" on a particular food after eating it frequently, and the Israelites had manna for breakfast, manna for lunch, and manna for dinner. If they wanted a snack between meals, it was manna. The manna could be baked, boiled, fried, and roasted; it could be mashed, toasted, and sliced—but it was still manna. I don't suppose there was much danger of the Israelites being overweight.

Maybe a few meals of manna would be fine, but forty years of manna? Of course, the people complained about this, and, one time, the Lord supplied some quail. But many of them died when they ate the quail. It wasn't because the food was tainted; it was because their hearts were tainted. (See Numbers 11:16–24; 31–34.) Finding an adequate supply of water was also a problem. The wilderness travelers often faced the lack of water; but God always came through, even with some miraculous demonstrations, in spite of their complaints. (See Exodus 15:23–25; 17:6; Numbers 20:8–11.) So, Caleb had a monotonous diet for forty years, and he didn't always know where he would get his next drink of water, but he never let it affect his attitude of faith.

Caleb never let the detour of a wilderness experience detour him from living in the supernatural. This giant of faith always kept his

Caleb was never moved from his position of life under the Son. He was diligent about keeping his heart in the right place.

attitude right with God. Although he wasn't living in the lap of luxury, and there was murmuring and rebellion all around, Caleb was never moved from his position of life under the Son. He was diligent about keeping his heart in the right place. Even though he had to wait and wait and wait for the promise, his spirit did not fail. Caleb's heart was established in God, and he was in for the long haul, no matter what length of time that took. Because Caleb's spirit never failed, his strength never failed.

Remember, God's Word tells us to guard our hearts with all diligence because the *"issues of life"* (Proverbs 4:23) come out of the heart. When Jesus said He had good news for the poor, He told the people that He was anointed to heal the brokenhearted. Again, healing begins in the heart. Jesus didn't first talk to the people about healing their bodies; He talked about healing their hearts. If the attitude of the heart is right, the body can be healthy. But if the heart attitude is wrong, the body is subject to sickness. Even if you receive a miraculous healing, you can lose it if your attitude is wrong. It all begins with a heart that is right toward God. The way to live life under the Son is to have a right attitude. With wrong attitudes, you will only live life under the sun.

Three Keys to Living Life Under the Son

What were the keys to Caleb's life that brought him through? What kept his attitude right? I found three basic things that were vital to his success.

Key #1. *Acknowledge the Supernatural Power of God*

First, Caleb had seen the miraculous demonstration of the power of God. As a young man, he had witnessed the ten plagues that spoiled Egypt and spared Israel. He had seen the Red Sea open for God's people and close over their enemies, and he had seen many Israelites healed when they ate the lamb. In the wilderness, Caleb's experiences with the miraculous had included drinking the "sweet" waters of Marah, drinking water that gushed out from a rock, and eating manna from heaven. This man had encountered the supernatural—he knew that life was more than natural.

Key #2. *Believe the Word*

Second, Caleb believed the Word. While most of the Israelites were people of natural provision, Caleb was a man who had faith in God's supernatural provision. God's Word didn't just go into Caleb's physical ears; it also went into his heart. He believed, according to Deuteronomy 33:25, that God would supply the necessary physical strength for every day he lived. At Marah, when the tree made the bitter water sweet, Caleb took to heart the revelation of Jehovah Rophe, "The Lord Your Health." God's promise to bring His people into a land flowing with milk and honey anchored the hope in Caleb's heart. I can just hear Caleb say, "I'm not going down the drain, because my health isn't going to fail, and neither is my strength." Caleb made a decision to stand firmly on God's promises and live in the supernatural, no matter what any of the doubters said.

Every time you have to make a decision, are you going to listen to other people or to God's promises? Of course, you are going to listen to God's promises. While the Bible does say there is safety in many counselors (see Proverbs 11:14), we are not to follow the advice of people whose suggestions are contrary to God's Word and ways. Allow God's promises to enter through your eyes and ears and drop into your heart. Then, you will walk in the supernatural and not be limited by the natural. Make one enormously important decision, and it will be your guide in making every other decision: Just like Caleb, decide to live according to the Word of God and His promises. Say, "I'm going to believe the promises, no matter what." People around you may not understand. They may not claim the promises; they may even try to explain them away. But those people will be living life under the sun, while you will enjoy life under the Son.

When we don't see God's answers right away, there is always a temptation to wonder how long we will have to wait. For Caleb, it was forty-five years—forty years in the desert and another five years during which he participated in battles taking various territories of the Israelites' inheritance in the Promised Land. (See Joshua 14:6–14.) Are you willing to wait forty-five years? Are you in for the long haul? Some people can't wait forty-five seconds, forty-five minutes, or even forty-five hours. Don't ask them to wait forty-five days and certainly not forty-five months. But forty-five years? Forget it! One seasoned evangelist has said that if you are willing to wait forever, it won't take very long! In other words, the longer you have any questions about the ability of God's

Word to bring your answer, the longer it will take. Caleb was convinced from the beginning, so he was able to wait forty-five years. God's Word doesn't wear out with the passing of time; it is always potent, full of supernatural power.

I find that God's Word just gets better and better. That's because God's unchanging Word is changing me and making me better! If you are absolutely convinced that God's Word works, you won't be moved by time or circumstance. Instead, the Word will move you into better circumstances in every area of

The Word will move you into better circumstances in every area of your life.

your life. The Word took Caleb into Canaan, didn't it? There, he finally received Hebron as his inheritance. He didn't waste time moaning and groaning about the lost years. At eighty-five, Caleb was able to conquer the giants and enjoy the remaining years of his life in the land that God had promised to him.

Key #3. Wholly Follow the Lord

The third key to Caleb's ability to live life under the Son came from the mouths of four people, including Caleb himself. First, God testified that He would give Caleb and his children the land upon which Caleb had walked, *"because he **wholly** followed the LORD"* (Deuteronomy 1:36). Second, Caleb's own words also testify of his faithfulness:

> *I was forty years old when Moses the ser-*
> *vant of the LORD sent me from Kadesh Bar-*
> *nea to spy out the land, and I brought back*
> *word to him as it was in my heart. Never-*
> *theless my brethren who went up with me*
> *made the heart of the people melt, but I*
> ***wholly*** *followed the LORD my God.*
> (Joshua 14:7–8)

Third, Moses swore to Caleb that the land where he had walked would be his because Caleb had *"wholly followed the LORD"* (Joshua 14:9). And fourth, Joshua wrote,

> *Hebron therefore became the inheritance of*
> *Caleb the son of Jephunneh the Kenizzite to*
> *this day, because he **wholly** followed the*
> *LORD God of Israel.* (Joshua 14:14)

Four times, we find the phrase *"wholly followed the LORD."* The word *wholly* comes from the word *whole* and means "complete," "entire," "full" or "total"; it is "without diminution." Caleb's heart was so full of the Word of God that his faith in the promises could never be diminished by doubt.

Caleb made a decision in his heart that he would serve the Lord with his entire being: his spirit, his mind, his emotions, his will, and his body. Some people want to serve God only with their minds. Give them an intellectual sermon or book, and they're fine; but if God doesn't speak to their intellect, forget it! If the mental "appetite" isn't being satisfied, they aren't satisfied. They know a lot *about* God, but that's it.

Others only "feel" God. These people are moved to serve the Lord only by emotional experience. If they don't have goose bumps or shivers up their spines, it just can't be God. They can dance and shout at church, but when the "high" is over, you can't find them. When people who run on emotion feel good, or when they have had an answer to prayer or have heard a great praise report, they "really love God." But when these people are at an emotional low, they may have a nervous breakdown.

Then, there are the people who will do anything physical for God. Their bodies are the only part of them in the service of the Lord. They think they aren't serving God unless they are involved in some physical activity. They will set up tables, move chairs, sweep floors, and climb ladders for God. All that is wonderful; but don't ask these people to come to a prayer meeting, read their Bibles every day, or study the Word.

Love for God should be our motivation for serving Him. God has told us to love and serve Him with all our hearts, with all our souls, with all our minds, and with all our strength. (See, for example, Mark 12:30.) That involves the whole person. God wants us to serve Him wholly. He knows that if we serve Him with only our minds, we will become warped. He knows that if we serve Him with only our emotions, we will get out of balance. And He knows that if we serve Him with only our bodies, all we will get are muscles unless our hearts are right. Don't ever think the path to heaven is paved with our "good" works.

God loves us so much that He wants us to be whole people. When we are whole people, we will be holy people. Without a holy walk, no person will see the Lord! (See Hebrews 12:14.) That means you must serve God with your mind. You may understand many things, but I guarantee that there will be things in life you won't understand. Are you going to throw away your faith when those things come along, or will you continue to be faithful? Some years ago, our entire church put every ounce of faith we had into believing for a lovely sixteen-year-old who had leukemia—and she died. Because of a circumstance they didn't understand, a few people decided it wasn't always God's will to heal. However, one person heard this word from the Lord: *Don't have questions about Me in this matter;* **you can't afford to doubt**. *My child is now with Me, but you are still on earth, where faith is the only way to live!*

> *God will come through for you, so hold on to your faith.*

What about your emotions? When you *feel* as if God is a million miles away and life is a downer, are you going to give up? No, your emotions belong to God when you are wholly committed to Him. If you feel upbeat, that's great. But if you feel down, it doesn't make any difference; God will come through for you, so hold on to your faith. Every one of us experiences disappointments, but don't give the enemy any opportunity in your life just because your emotions are on a roller coaster. Command your emotions to get in line with God's Word and remain steady!

A young woman who used to work in our ministry married a man who seemed to be a totally committed Christian. However, as soon as they were married, things began to go sour, and he became a different person—angry, verbally abusive, and delinquent. Instead of falling apart, she took a stand of faith. When the situation seemed utterly hopeless and her emotions screamed for attention, she stood on God's promises. Eventually, the couple separated, and he took employment in another city. But she didn't let go when she had every earthly reason to "hang it up." Nearly two years went by, but she never gave up hope. Then, the husband came back to talk his wife into a divorce. Before he left, however, he had recommitted his life to the Lord, and the marriage was restored. He said, "I never thought she would stick it out; but she is a woman of faith, not a woman of feelings." Praise the Lord! This husband is now wholly serving God, and he has been healed of the emotional abuse he suffered as a child.

Are we going to be fair-weather Christians and serve our bodies instead of the Lord? Some people are into "works," but others are into comfort. Of course, they are in church—unless they are tired or the weather is bad. If you aren't feeling well, where do you belong? No, you don't belong in bed; you belong in church, where you can receive prayer for healing! Let me tell you about a situation that really touched my heart. A young Christian woman, full of life and vitality, was hit by a drunken driver, and she came out of the accident a paraplegic. Her mate didn't leave her as some do; instead, he remained wholly dedicated to her and to the Lord. He works and does the housework and the cooking; he feeds, bathes, and dresses her, and the two of them attend every service at their church. Yes, they are believing for her healing; but, in the meantime, they are wholly serving the Lord!

Again, when I look at Caleb, I see that he kept his attitude right. He never had a nervous breakdown, and he never wore out physically. With his mind, his emotions, and his body, Caleb wholly served the Lord. Let's look at the outcome of the life of this holy man.

God says that His thoughts toward us are good and not evil, so that He may give us a good future. (See Jeremiah 29:11.) Although Jeremiah had not yet penned those words, Caleb knew the truth of them, and he wholly trusted the Lord with his future. As I wrote earlier, when Israel entered Canaan, Caleb asked Joshua for the land of Hebron, where he had walked forty-five years earlier. This man knew God's promise to give him the land upon which he had walked.

Caleb lived life in the supernatural and not in the natural. That's the way God expects every one of us to live!

This mountainous country was the home of the giants. Undaunted, Caleb said that he was as strong at eighy-five as he had been at forty, and if the Lord would be with him, he would drive out every giant. (See Joshua 14:11.) Joshua granted Caleb's request, and Caleb went up and took Hebron. Caleb didn't go part of the way; he went all the way. This man knew how to live life under the Son, because he was wholly committed to God. He lived life in the supernatural and not in the natural. That's the way God expects every one of us to live! We can all experience life *under the Son* instead of life *under the sun* when we wholly belong to the Lord.

Ways to Wholly Serve the Lord

Let's look at ways in which we can wholly serve the Lord, as Caleb did.

Wholly Believe

Caleb wholly believed; like Abraham, he did not stagger at God's promise. (See Romans 4:20 KJV.) You, too, must fully believe as you wholly follow Him. Remember, if your mind belongs to the Lord, you can renew your mind with the Word of God and have the mind of Christ. (See Romans 12:2; 1 Corinthians 2:16.) You don't have to become senile; your mind can remain strong and healthy. Every change in your life can be a change for the better when your emotions are wholly God's. When you wholly commit your body to the Lord, you don't have to conform to the world; you will be conformed to God. Quit accepting the natural and step into the supernatural!

Wholly Witness

Caleb wholly witnessed with his life. Everything Caleb did and said was a witness of his wholeness. His life was constant and unswerving. When the crowd would have stoned him for insisting they could take Canaan, he didn't say, "Put down that rock; maybe I'm wrong." There was no compromise in Caleb's life. He didn't care if it was a crowd of unbelievers or a crowd of giants, he didn't swerve from God's Word. Our lives also should wholly witness Christ. People should know that we are Christians. They should see a difference in our lifestyle. We should radiate such love that others want what we have. Are we as eager to share Jesus now as when we first met Him, or have we become sophisticated cowards who hide behind a myriad of excuses? Every person we meet is either on the way to heaven or on the way to hell! Jesus gave His life for them; have we wholly given our lives to Him?

Wholly Wait

Then, Caleb wholly waited. For forty-five years, he kept his eyes on Hebron. He had supernatural eyesight. In the natural, he could see snakes, desert, whining people, and manna, but he kept his eyes on what he *knew* was ahead. If we are to come into God's expected future for us, we must also keep our eyes on God's Word. Giants challenged Caleb, but they didn't prevent him from taking Hebron. Jewish history says that when the giants saw this eighty-five-year-old man, they *retired*. Later, Caleb *gave* Hebron as an offering to the Lord for a "city of refuge," although he kept the surrounding land. There is no doubt that we live in challenging times, but we can "retire" every giant the devil brings our way, whether we are twenty-five or eighty-five—when we wholly wait on God. I like it when our faith scares the devil! Is your life an offering to the Lord?

Every Bit Whole in Him

Did you know that *Hebron* means "fellowship"? It is interesting that Caleb obtained Hebron after years of continual fellowship with God. That same kind of fellowship with God can be yours when you wholly follow the Lord. That means that, day by day, you must be consistent with God in every area of your life. Each day, look to Him and say, "I'm wholly Yours, Lord: my spirit, my soul, and my body are Yours." If one day brings a defeat or

Daily remember that God will take every situation you give to Him and turn it to your good.

a disappointment, use it as an opportunity to gain another victory that will glorify the Lord. Daily remember that God will take every situation you give to Him and turn it to your good. (See Romans 8:28.) After a while, this way of living becomes a habit. It's not a struggle; instead, it is spontaneous! Then, you will realize you are every bit whole in Him—spirit, soul, and body. You are no longer living life *under the sun*. Now, you are living life *under the Son!* It's God's victorious lifestyle for those who are wholly committed to Him.

8

Root It Up

The doctor stood at the woman's bedside, shaking his head in disbelief. The facts were incredible; nevertheless, every test revealed no cancer in this woman's body. Two weeks ago, the patient had been given only another twenty-four hours to live. Her husband had completed funeral arrangements, and the family had been notified. However, everything had changed since then. The happy doctor was looking now into the bright, smiling face of a woman who was very much alive. Although there was no medical explanation for what had happened, the cancer was gone, and she was being discharged! The medical chart read, "Cancer in remission."

Everyone involved in this situation was baffled by the woman's mysterious healing—except one individual who believed in God's marvelous power to heal. This person had never met the dying woman, but she had heard of the woman's plight through a friend. Fierce anger and intense, biblical hope (confident expectation) had risen up inside her like a geyser—anger at the devil's disease and strong faith in God's ability to heal. There was no question in her mind as to either Satan's intention or God's intention. Jesus defined both purposes when He said, *"The thief does not come except to steal, and to kill, and to destroy. I have come that they may have life, and that they may have it more abundantly"* (John 10:10).

The woman prayed, "You foul spirit of cancer, leave this woman's body. I curse you in Jesus' name, and I command this cancer to die at the roots. It shall find no place in this body to stay." Within the critical twenty-four hours, the "dying" woman reported to her friend that she could feel something moving about in her body. Even the friend could feel the movement when she placed her hands on the woman's abdomen. This was strange, indeed, but the woman was feeling better. In a day or two, the patient began to vomit large quantities of some odd substance. When the vomiting ceased, the woman began a remarkable recovery. All the doctors could say when the lab tests came back clear was, "She vomited the cancer from her body."

Rooting Up What God Didn't Plant

This amazing recovery came to my attention because the lady who had prayed was a friend of mine. I know the facts surrounding this case seem unbelievable, but so does the record of Jesus' encounter with a fig tree in Mark 11:12–21. Let me refresh your memory. One day, Jesus was hungry, so He decided to eat fruit from the fig tree. When He found no figs, He spoke to the tree, saying, *"Let no one eat fruit from you ever again"* (verse 14). The next day, Jesus' disciples were astonished to see that the fig tree was dead, *dried up from the roots.* Peter said, *"Rabbi, look! The fig tree which You* **cursed** *has withered away"* (verse 21).

You may say, "Well, that was Jesus; He can do anything." Look at Jesus' response to His disciples:

> *So Jesus answered and said to them, "Have faith in God. For assuredly, I say to you,* **whoever says** *to this mountain, 'Be removed and be cast into the sea,'* **and does not doubt** *in his heart,* **but believes** *that those things he says will be done,* **he will have whatever he says."** (Mark 11:22–23)

Jesus has given power to believers, if they do not doubt but believe what they say, to curse roots and move mountains. Are you a believer, or are you a doubter?

Jesus and His disciples were near the Mount of Olives when He spoke that promise, but we know He doesn't expect us to go around cursing tree roots or moving mountains—unless they are in the way of God's purpose. He does expect us

In the authority of Jesus' name, we can root up sickness, disease, infirmity, and all manner of evil, which our Lord certainly has not planted.

to root up problems (such as cancer) and to move the mountains of difficulty in our lives. Jesus said, *"Every plant which My heavenly Father has not planted will be* **uprooted**" (Matthew 15:13). We can begin by rooting up our personal fears and doubts. We do this by planting the faith-producing Word in our hearts. Then, in the authority of Jesus' name, we can root up sickness, disease, infirmity, and all manner of evil, which our Lord certainly has not planted.

Incidentally, in case you have any question about "mountain-moving" faith, I must tell you this true story. A missionary in India taught at a girls' school that was located under the shadow of a mountain. The sun never reached the girls' dormitory; consequently, it was cold and dank, and their laundry wouldn't dry properly. One day, the missionary taught on the passage in Mark 11. Right then, the students decided to believe that "their" mountain would be removed. The girls prayed with great expectancy, although their teacher didn't encourage them because she didn't want their faith crushed. In just a few days, the astonished missionary saw giant earthmovers taking huge "bites" from the mountain that was in the way of a government project. The mountain was removed, but Jesus' little disciples were not surprised.

We are to have faith in God's ability, not our own. In the Scriptures, we read that God's commission overwhelmed the prophet Jeremiah. At the time, the young man considered himself to be only a "child" who could not speak for the Lord with any measure of authority. However, the Lord set him straight:

> *But the* L<small>ORD</small> *said to me: "Do not say, 'I am a youth,' for you shall go to all to whom I send you, and whatever I command you, you shall speak."...Then the* L<small>ORD</small> *put forth His hand and touched my mouth, and the* L<small>ORD</small> *said to me: "Behold, I have put **My words in your mouth**. See, I have this day set you over the nations and over the kingdoms, **to root out** and to pull down, to destroy and to throw down, **to build and to plant**."*
> (Jeremiah 1:7, 9–10)

Jeremiah became a mighty mouthpiece for God. God used him to root out and expose much evil in Israel and to be a witness for righteousness.

One of the most interesting testimonies that has come in to our ministry was from a man who lives in South Dakota. He farms the same land his father and grandfather and great-grandfather farmed before him. So, the land has belonged to his family for four generations, but before that it belonged to the Indians from whom it had been purchased. Every year, the farmer battled a poisonous weed that would kill the cattle if they ate very much of it. At best, the weed made the cattle quite ill. This little weed was costing the man a great deal of money because the land had to be sprayed by a crop duster every season.

Despite all this effort, the root system of the poisonous plant was never killed. Then, when studying the history of the area, the farmer discovered that long ago, the Indians had put a curse on the land. Being Christians, the farmer and his wife began to fast and pray to break this curse. The two of them would drive around their property and command the root system of the weeds to die. There was no change for a season or two, but the farmer and his wife stood firm and didn't give up. The couple kept trusting God and confessing that the poisonous weeds were dead at the roots.

One spring morning, the farmer's young son went out and pulled up one of the weeds, which were already growing again. The plant looked as though it had been thriving—but *the roots were shriveled and dry.* Every weed they examined was the same way; they had all died at the roots. Although the neighboring farmers continued to battle the obnoxious weed, this man never had the weeds on his property again. You see, Jesus said that everything that wasn't planted by God would be rooted up. Most assuredly, the poisonous weed was not planted by God. This man believed the promise and acted accordingly. Now he is rid of the costly nuisance.

Let me tell you that if you have cancer, it didn't come from God. If you are sick or disabled with any kind of condition, God did not plant that thing in your life. If God didn't plant the destructive thing, then who did, and what are you supposed to do about it? Satan is the one who sows the weeds, and the weeds need to be pulled. (See Matthew 13:28, 30.) Whatever weed is in your life, root it up! Get a hold of that weed with the Word of God on your tongue. Curse it at the roots, and it has to die. Just like the weeds on the farmer's land, it may not die instantly, but it will happen. The tree Jesus cursed at the roots showed no immediate signs of death, but a day later, it was dead.

Common Questions about Healing

I now want to answer some questions that are often asked in regard to the subject of healing. We have touched on several of these points previously, but they are necessary to repeat in this context and are worth our attention. If I root out doubts you may have concerning healing, then I can plant good seeds of faith in your heart. My goal is to enable you to believe that anything is possible with God.

Is Faith Necessary for Healing?

Faith is the issue of the first question. Is some faith always needed in order for a person to be healed? Earlier in the book, we looked at some circumstances when it wasn't apparent that faith was present in the individual who was healed, but we can't say there wasn't someone exercising faith. For example, no one knew someone was exercising faith for the woman dying of cancer. Her cure was unexplainable to all those concerned. Nevertheless, mighty faith was in operation.

> But let him ask in faith, with no doubting, for he who doubts is like a wave of the sea driven and tossed by the wind. For let not that man suppose that he will receive anything from the Lord; he is a double-minded man, unstable in all his ways.
>
> (James 1:6–8)

The book of James tells us that any individual who wavers between faith and doubt can never really believe in order to receive. Remember that Jesus Himself could do no mighty works in His hometown because of the people's unbelief. That unbelief became a strong wall that even Jesus' power could not penetrate. It wasn't that power wasn't present, but faith was not present in most of those in Nazareth. Only a few sickly people were healed. The original text indicates that only minor ailments were cured. (See Mark 6:1–6.)

> *The power to heal is released when two or more agree in faith.*

Paul perceived that a crippled man in Lystra had faith to be healed. (See Acts 14:8–10.) I'm certain there were numerous cripples in Lystra; and, if Paul's compassion could have healed them, they all would have gotten up and walked. However, only one man was made whole when he mixed faith with the Word that Paul preached. Then, there was an agreement of faith. When Paul commanded the cripple to stand, the man's feet and legs received strength, and he leaped and walked. This connection of faith produced great results, because the power to heal is released when two or more agree *in faith*. (See Matthew 18:19.)

Several people agreed in faith for their friend whom Jesus healed when they lowered him through a roof into Jesus' presence. (See Mark 2:3–12.) Additional examples of people who came to Jesus on behalf of others included the father with the dying daughter (see, for example, Mark 5:22–24, 35–43) and the centurion with the dying servant (see, for example, Matthew 8:5–10, 13). We could list others, but in every case, Jesus said the healing resulted when someone had faith in His healing power. Still others believed when no one around could "see" what they saw with eyes of faith. There was the woman with the flow of blood, blind Bartimaeus, and Peter and John, who had faith for the healing of the lame man at the temple gate. I like to think of God's power as a stick of dynamite and faith as the fire that lights it. Incidentally, one Greek word translated *"power"* in the New Testament is *dunamis*, from which we get the word *dynamite*.

I know there have been times when God has told me to use my faith for someone who didn't have faith. These people were often so tired and weary that their faith was completely drained, but I would tell them to lean on my faith, and they were healed. When they were unable to ignite the dynamite, I had the match, and together we released God's power. Whether it is one's own faith or faith "by proxy" that connects with the Lord's power to heal, it is still faith. When God's Word lets us know that we can't please Him without faith (see Hebrews 11:6), then I must conclude that faith is of vital importance when it comes to healing. Jesus said, *"Whatever things you ask when you pray, believe that you receive them, and you will have them"* (Mark 11:24).

For what reason would anyone who loves Jesus want to neglect faith? Well, the enemy comes in and plants seeds of doubt in people's minds to make them think they can never have the kind of faith necessary for healing. Those seeds sprout and grow roots that need to be pulled. Sometimes, faith wears thin during a severe trial when the answer doesn't come immediately, and discouraged people become weak in faith. However, faith can always be encouraged by others and renewed through the Word of God. God's promises are a never-ending source of supply, so His children don't have to run dry.

One evening, a gentleman in our congregation was having severe pain in his feet, and he stood for healing prayer. After the service, his feet hurt worse than they had before. Did the man say, "Well, I guess it isn't going to work for me"? No, indeed! Although the man could scarcely stand due to the pain, he kept standing on the Word of God. For a week, the man continued to tell his feet they were healed. In the next service he attended, I received a word of knowledge about someone's feet being healed, and it was for this man. He later testified that his feet were healed at that moment. The problem was rooted out and the pain was gone.

This story reminds me of an evangelist who was doing a seminar on healing—but he could barely get to the platform because of severe pain from a plantar wart on his foot. How embarrassing! He prayed and prayed, but nothing happened. He complained to God about the matter...nothing. He reminded God that this should be embarrassing to Him, too...still nothing. One day, after a service, the man was in agony, and the Lord said to him, *Ask that young man over there to pray for your foot.*

Now, this young man was mentally disabled, so the evangelist argued with God. The Lord said, *Fine, it's your foot!* You can guess the outcome—he surrendered, the young man prayed, and the foot was healed. In telling the story later, the evangelist said, "The devil *planted* that plantar wart, but through humble faith, God rooted it out."

Does God Heal Children of Unsaved Parents?

Do children of unsaved parents get healed? Does God heal sinners? Yes, the unsaved are often healed in meetings where the atmosphere is charged with faith. Of course, the sinner also may have exercised a measure of faith by attending the meeting. I've known unbelievers to be healed when people of faith prayed for them. The person prayed for may have been a spouse, a child, another loved one, or a neighbor. Those who receive healing may go out and sin some more, but they can never forget that God healed them. They have had an encounter with God and His power that can't be denied. I believe the Lord will eventually reach those sinners. The entire family of one of our pastors was born again when an unsaved grandmother was miraculously healed by God.

Although I believe that children of unsaved parents can be healed when someone of faith prays for them, I know that most of the time, children are not healed when their parents are unbelievers. God has made parents responsible for their innocent offspring, and if there is no one to believe, how can healing take place? This is tragic but true. Children don't know to

have faith unless they have met Jesus through someone. I've even heard of children having visions of Jesus; but I believe that either someone was praying for
them, or they were reaching out to God. There is no
question that children are very dear to God's heart.

King David lost his first son by Bathsheba because his sin had *"made the enemies of the LORD show
utter contempt"* (2 Samuel 12:14 NIV). Jeroboam, who
was first to rule the northern kingdom of Israel, also
lost a child because of sin in his life. This man set
up a terrible system of idolatry in his nation in order
to keep the men of Israel from attending the feasts
at the Jerusalem temple in the southern kingdom of
Judah. The king feared losing the men's allegiance,
so he pulled them away from their allegiance to God.
Jeroboam turned from the Lord when he became
nervous about losing a kingdom that God had given
to him. This man didn't realize he was sacrificing his
own son for a kingdom.

When King Jeroboam's son became critically ill,
the king was frantic. Like most parents, he loved his
son. The distraught king had his queen disguise herself and go to a prophet to ask if the child would live.
The old blind prophet Ahijah, who had prophesied
that Jeroboam would rule Israel, knew by the Spirit
of God that it was the queen. The Lord had already
given Ahijah a message for her:

> *Arise therefore, go to your own house. When
> your feet enter the city, the child shall die.
> And all Israel shall mourn for him and bury
> him, for he is the only one of Jeroboam who*

shall come to the grave, **because in him there is found something good toward the Lord God of Israel in the house of Jeroboam.** (1 Kings 14:12–13)

That seems like a strange message, doesn't it? The child was going to die because God saw something good in him. Let's examine this situation. God loved this child in whom He saw goodness. Therefore, he didn't want Jeroboam's son to grow up in a household of sin and become an idolater. God did not intervene to heal the child, and so the child died. I don't want you to misunderstand me here. God *did not* put the illness on Jeroboam's son. In order to do that, God would have had to borrow sickness from the devil. Nevertheless, while this precious child was still innocent, God delivered him from the evil influence and took the child to Himself. This good boy was spared an eternity in hell.

Jeroboam's son died because of the sins of his father and mother. Parents who are ungodly can bring tragedy, sickness, and death upon their own children. The Scriptures say that the sins of the fathers are visited on the children to at least the third and fourth generations. (See Numbers 14:18.) This is a terrible truth, but what can children learn in ungodly homes but ungodliness? However, youngsters brought up in the nurture and admonition of the Lord learn godliness. Blessings follow their generations. If you are a parent, I'm going to tell you that your faith can heal your children; your lack of faith can kill your children. Don't blame the death of a child on God. God is not a baby killer.

I believe that the Lord is particularly interested in the precious life of innocent children. Jesus said,

Take heed that you do not despise one of these little ones, for I say to you that in heaven their angels always see the face of My Father who is in heaven.

(Matthew 18:10)

Three of the gospel writers recorded Jesus' awesome words of warning when He said that if anyone offends a child who believes in Him, or causes that child to sin, it would be better for that person to have a millstone hung around his neck and then be thrown into the sea to drown. (See, for example, Luke 17:1–3 NKJV, NIV.)

God delights to heal children when they are sick, but someone needs to have faith on their behalf.

If the Lord cares so much for children, then He is certainly ready to heal them. God delights to heal children when they are sick, but someone needs to have faith on their behalf. The Lord has entrusted these little lives into the hands of parents who are responsible for training and molding them, as well as protecting them from both natural and spiritual evil. What normal parents would not want to provide for their children and keep them healthy when it is within their power to do so? God the Father is no different with His children, especially the little ones who are so vulnerable.

When the Syro-Phoenician woman—a Gentile—came to Jesus and asked Him to heal her demonized daughter, Jesus told her that healing was *"the children's bread"* (Mark 7:27). The children to whom Jesus referred were the descendants of Abraham, to whom Jesus came first. (See verse 27 and Matthew 15:24.) Nevertheless, this undaunted woman, who was considered a "dog" by the Jews, said that even little puppies can eat the crumbs that fall from the table. She was willing to pick up a few "crumbs off the floor" for her daughter. Although she wasn't a Jew, Jesus honored her persistent faith, and the child was healed.

Parents, it is your job to provide "healing bread" for your children, just as this mother provided healing bread for her daughter. We need to believe the Lord for our children's healing. Where there is no faith involved, there is sickness and premature death. Of course, we need to teach our children about healing. They need to learn the Scriptures that promise healing to them. Children so readily believe what they are taught—let's make sure we teach them righteousness. Yet, where there is much sin involved, a child may die while he or she is still innocent and be removed from the awful contamination of sin.

Once a Person Is Healed, Can Sickness Return?

Can an affliction come back on a person who was really healed? Third John 2 gives us a clue:

*Beloved, I pray that you may prosper in all things and be in health, **just as your soul prospers**.*

Health and healing are tied in with soul prosperity. Your mind must be established on the Word of God, your emotions must be controlled by the Lord, and your choices must be made according to God's principles. That is living in soul prosperity. Anything else brings sickness to the soul and sickness to the body.

The devil is always lurking in the wings, looking for opportunities to do anything he can to harm you. He will gladly put sickness back on your body if you give him the chance to do so. Affliction can come back when a person begins to walk with the devil instead of walking with the Lord. Anyone who gets out of faith is open for another attack of the enemy. Unless you continue to live in soul prosperity, the enemy can come back. Jesus overcame Satan's temptations with the Word of God, and that is the same way you need to resist him. Of course, Jesus was living a life of righteousness, and so must you. Does that mean you must never sin to stay healed? No, but you must repent of known sin in your life. Go to the mirror of God's Word, and it will show you any sin.

John 5:5–15 tells of a man whom Jesus healed of an *"infirmity"* that had totally incapacitated him for thirty-eight years. The Lord's healing power was so mighty that it instantly drove out an affliction that had bound this man for nearly four decades. Nevertheless, Jesus told the man, *"Sin no more, lest a worse thing come upon you"* (verse 14). Jesus was telling the man that sin would open the door to more sickness.

Do you recall that Jesus forgave the sins of the man lowered through a roof before He healed the man's body? Jesus knew that the man needed to live in soul prosperity so he could live in physical prosperity. Don't you know that man thought twice before he ever again indulged in sin!

Jesus described how evil spirits can enter a person who once was delivered:

> *When an unclean spirit goes out of a man, he goes through dry places, seeking rest; and finding none, he says, "I will return to my house from which I came." And when he comes, he finds it swept and put in order. Then he goes and takes with him seven other spirits more wicked than himself, and they enter and dwell there; and the last state of that man is worse than the first.*
> (Luke 11:24–26)

What was Jesus saying here? For one thing, He told us that demons seek residence in people. These demons can have their bags packed with all sorts of disease and infirmity. Jesus healed a woman with a *"spirit of infirmity"* (Luke 13:11) who had been bent over for eighteen years, and He said the woman should be *"loosed from this bond"* (verse 16) of Satan.

Specifically, Jesus told about the man with the demons to illustrate that if we do not fill ourselves with the Word of God after we are free, something much worse can happen to us. Although the man in Jesus' illustration was clean, he was also empty. By not filling the empty space with God, he had hung a "vacancy" sign on himself. The demon and his companions were waiting for the opportunity to enter the man and gain a stronghold. Then, the man was in worse condition than before. You cannot be a spiritual vacuum; either you will fill your soul with the spiritual things of God, or Satan will fill you with things from his spirit realm. Never forget that if the devil can find a place in you, he will take it!

When God says in Nahum 1:9 that *"affliction will not rise up a second time,"* we should understand two things: (1) sickness may try to return, but (2) it is never the Lord's will for this to happen. Jesus paid an awful price for our healing; and it should be obvious that God not only wants to heal His people but also wants them to stay healed and continue to live in health. When Jesus healed the boy who was having seizures, He said, *"Deaf and dumb spirit, I command you, come out of him and **enter him no more!**"* (Mark 9:25). You have the power in Jesus' name to tell sickness and disease that it cannot come back again! When I receive healing, I tell the devil that he will never put that sickness back on me, and then I quote Nahum 1:9 to him. Satan probably knows the Word better than I do; but I remind him that I know it, too, and I know that it works.

> *God not only wants to heal His people but also wants them to stay healed and continue to live in health.*

When young David knocked down Goliath, he finished the job by cutting off the giant's head. He was taking no chance that his enemy would get back up. I guarantee you that Goliath certainly wasn't going anyplace without his head—not on his own power, anyway. When you knock down the devil, cut off his head! Tell him that there is no way he is going to bring that affliction back to you, and that he isn't bringing any other affliction, either. It grieves me when people get healed of cancer, and then, six months or a year later, they die. Doctors find absolutely no cancer cells in these patients; they are in total remission, and yet cancer attacks them again. We can stop this sort of thing, and we must stop it in Jesus' name.

Some people tell me they have a history of some condition or another, or they say some physical problem has been passed through their family for generations. I don't care about the past history; I'm concerned with the future. Stop that evil thing and pass it back to the devil. If he wants to play ball, show him you're on the winning team! God didn't plant sinus trouble in your life or cancer or heart disease or back problems. Root them out with the Word of God and stand guard over your property:

> So you shall serve the Lord your God, and He will bless your bread and your water. And I will take sickness away from the midst of you.   (Exodus 23:25)

You see, there is a condition to soul prosperity and healing that lasts; *it is found in serving the Lord.*

Can We Use "Points of Contact" to Heal?

Some people ask, "What about things like anointing oil, prayer cloths, the laying on of hands, and touching a TV? Do these things have the power to heal? And what is their purpose?"

When our ministry sends out letters containing prayer cloths, I've noticed that we get more response than at any other time. Testimony after testimony of miraculous healing comes flooding back to us. We also get the most critical mail at this time because there are many folks who do not understand this sort of thing. They think it is just a very unspiritual gimmick.

But what about the testimony of the Scriptures? Naaman was healed of leprosy when he dipped in the Jordan seven times. God answered Gideon through a sheepskin, and Hezekiah through a sundial. People were healed when the shadow of Peter fell on them; pieces of cloth taken from Paul's body healed others. Even the Lord Jesus used a "gimmick" when He put "spitballs" on a blind man's eyes and then told him to go wash them off. You can't knock results; the man was healed! And what about the laying on of hands commanded by Jesus, and the anointing with oil spoken of by James? We need to find the practical truth here that will help our understanding of these unusual practices that can be aids to healing.

God tells us in Psalm 103:14 that He knows our *"frame"*; He understands that our bodies are made of dust. May I add that the five senses are physical, experienced in the body? We all very much see, hear, taste, smell, and touch. Is it so unusual, then, that the Lord would involve our senses in order to effect healing in our bodies? I think it is just like God to get the spirit, the soul, and the body working together in healing. If our senses are so unspiritual, then why did the Lord give them to us? It's the way we use our senses that can bring unspirituality and sin. No doubt our senses can tantalize us to sin, but they can also draw us to God. Doesn't Psalm 19:1 say, *"The heavens declare the glory of God; and the firmament shows His handiwork"*? How are you going to know they are there if you can't see them?

I suppose one of the most criticized of all aids to healing is "Put your hand on the TV." Can a television heal anyone, even if a person greatly used by God to heal the sick is speaking on the "tube"? If the TV could heal, all we'd need to do is set up TVs in churches and tell people to touch them. Then, what does happen when people receive healing in this manner? The TV is simply a *point of contact* for faith. Faith seems to rise in people when their senses are involved through some point of contact, but they are not healed by TVs, prayer cloths, oil, or hands. However, there is a holy anointing on any such item when it has been consecrated to the Lord for the purpose of healing.

Our church youth pastor was suffering so badly with a sinus infection that he stayed home from work one day. While he was home, he took the opportunity to watch a man on TV who had a healing ministry. At one point, this man said, "If you are suffering in your body right now, touch your TV and believe with me for your healing." The pastor thought, *What do I have to lose? I'm so miserable, I'll do it.* At the very moment he put his hands on the TV, the minister said, "There's someone watching who is suffering terribly with a severe sinus infection, and that person is being healed right now." Our youth pastor felt the power of God go through him, and instantly his sinus passages began to drain. He was at work the next day!

> *Probably the most effective point of contact in healing is the laying on of hands.*

Probably the most effective point of contact in healing is the laying on of hands. I have seen more people healed when others laid hands on them than any other way. Many times, when I have laid hands on people who were sick, I think I felt worse than they did. Nevertheless, they received their healing. It wasn't my healthy hands that healed them. However, my hands were a faith contact for those individuals. I had faith for their healing, based on the Word of God, and they believed they would be healed when I put my hands on them. Sometimes, when these people were healed, I received my healing, as well. Why? Because the prayer of faith, coupled with their healing, strengthened my faith to be healed. Folks, don't put God in a box; allow Him to flow according to His will.

Can the Devil Heal People?

Another question people have is, "Can the devil heal? Does he have the power to heal sick bodies?" One time, when Jesus cast a demon out of a person, some of the bystanders accused Him of doing it by the power of Satan. They said, *"He casts out demons by Beelzebub, the ruler of the demons"* (Luke 11:15). Jesus answered,

> *Every kingdom divided against itself is brought to desolation, and a house divided against a house falls. If Satan also is divided against himself, how will his kingdom stand? Because you say I cast out demons by Beelzebub....But if I cast out demons with the finger of God, surely the kingdom of God has come upon you.*
>
> (Luke 11:17–18, 20)

Jesus made it quite clear that Satan would be tearing apart his own kingdom if he were to do any good work, such as healing or casting out demons. Satan's kingdom is full of sickness, death, and destruction, not health, life, and prosperity. Jesus said good things belong to God's kingdom.

Examine the book of Job, and you will find that it was not God who brought all the calamity into Job's life; *it was the devil.* (See Job 1:12.) It is often debated whether God removed the protective hedge around Job, or Job removed it himself through fear or self-righteousness. I just know the Lord allowed Satan the opportunity to attack Job. Nevertheless, God called Job an upright man who feared God and hated evil. (See Job 1:8; 2:3.) In the trial, Job never cursed God (see Job 1:22; 2:9–10), and, in the end, God blessed Job with twice as much as he had before. (See Job 42:10.)

James 1:13–15 instructs us never to accuse God of being the author of temptations in our lives, because His acts are never evil. Then, it says,

Every good gift and every perfect gift is from above, and comes down from the Father of lights, with whom there is no variation or shadow of turning.   (verse 17)

Just as there is never any change in God, there is never any change in the devil. Satan is *always* the bearer of bad tidings, such as sickness and disease, while God is *always* the bearer of good tidings, such as healing and health! The book of James does tell us that people are led into temptation when they succumb to their own lusts. Beware that you do not give Satan opportunity in your life.

Jesus said He came to undo all the works of the devil: *"God anointed Jesus of Nazareth with the Holy Spirit and with power, who went about doing good and healing all who were oppressed by the devil, for God was with Him"* (Acts 10:38). The infallible Word says Jesus is the Healer and the devil is the oppressor. Don't ever allow Satan to confuse you on this point.

We often hear or read about miraculous healings that have come from fountains or mountains, visions or apparitions. Let me say again that if the healing isn't being done by the power of the only true God in the name of His Son Jesus Christ of Nazareth, then there is something wrong at the root of the thing, no matter how good it may seem. When you're confused by these things, get to the root. If God hasn't planted it, it doesn't have good roots. If Jesus isn't glorified as God manifested in the flesh, then a counterfeit work is being performed by Satan. Always find where Jesus fits into the picture.

Remember that Satan can come disguised as an angel of light (see 2 Corinthians 11:14 NASB), and Paul said not to believe if even an angel came preaching "another" gospel (see Galatians 1:8).

It is possible that some of these people have had true angelic visitations, and I know of verified instances when people have seen Jesus. Yet, although there are scriptural accounts of angelic visitations in which the people who saw them were unaware of their true identity (see Hebrews 13:2), I know of no instance when these heavenly messengers brought healing.

On the basis of Scripture, I do know it is impossible for someone who is dead to appear to the living, no matter how venerated that person may have been. In Luke 16:19–31, Jesus told about a rich man in hell who pleaded with Abraham to send the beggar Lazarus from paradise to warn the rich man's ungodly brothers of their impending doom. However, the rich man was told that the living must accept God's Word to receive salvation. Jesus was restating the teaching of the Old Testament that we must seek God's direction, not the spirits of the dead. (See Deuteronomy 18:9–14; Isaiah 8:19.)

Why Do Some People Die Prematurely?

Finally, what about the people who die short of their length of days? Do we have any answers? Well, in some instances, I believe those who die as a result of illness get a glimpse of heaven, and they choose to stay there. I've heard testimonies of men and women who've had death experiences and did not want to return, but, because someone was praying for them fervently and effectively, the Lord sent them back. Some die because they have become so tired and weakened in the struggle to live that they have found themselves unable to continue in the fight of faith.

I am aware of a well-known pastor who lost a battle with cancer, but a personal friend of his told me that the man wanted to go on home. As we have seen, children may die because of unbelieving parents, some die because they are in the realm of fear and doubt, and others die because they are not walking in soul prosperity. Still others die, and none of us this side of eternity will ever know why; but we don't quit trusting God. Job had no idea that it was Satan who brought all his trouble, but he could still say of God, "Though He slay me, yet will I trust Him" (Job 13:15).

> *The more accurately the body of Christ walks in the power of God, the more we see healing take place.*

We can't deny that people who receive prayer for healing are not always healed; they may even die. I don't have all the answers, and neither does any other person, but I'm not going to stop praying and believing the Lord to touch people with His healing power. If I saw only a few people receive their healings or be raised from their deathbeds, I'd still keep praying for the sick. It is a scriptural thing to do, and I'm happy to report that we continually see more healed than are not healed! The more accurately the body of Christ walks in the power of God, the more we see healing take place. Don't ever allow what looks like a failure to dampen your zeal to pray a healing prayer for yourself or others. Remember, according to James 5:15, the prayer of faith will save (deliver, redeem, and heal) the sick, and the Lord will raise them up!

9

Name That Problem

It was "only" a dream, but it was a spiritual dream with a profound meaning. My friend knew the moment she awakened that the Lord had a message for her. In the dream, this woman was teaching a group of people. During the time of instruction, she raised her arm and pointed to a "whatnot" shelf on the wall where there were a number of objects. When she did this, everything on the shelf began to shake and rattle; but, in a few moments, they all became still. Again the woman raised her arm and pointed at one particular object on the shelf. This time, the object to which she pointed lifted from the shelf, moved across the room suspended in midair, and came to rest in her outstretched hand. As the lady pondered the events in the dream, the Lord made quite clear what He wanted her to know: Be specific when you pray, and you will get specific results.

How to Pray Specific Prayers

I want to say that same thing to you now: "Be specific when you pray, and you will get specific results!" Broad, general prayers, which I call "generic" prayers, may shake things a little, but they don't bring results. If you pray for nothing in particular, that's exactly what you'll get—nothing in particular! The more specifically you use your faith, the more specific the results will be. It is very important to identify the problem or situation on which you use your faith. Be specific in the way you pray, and be specific about what you pray. Both are very important.

> *The more specifically you use your faith, the more specific the results will be.*

There was an old TV show called *Name That Tune*. You may remember it. On the program, the player who guessed the title of the "mystery" tune received a prize. Only a fragment of an obscure song was played for the contestant, and so it was quite difficult to win the prize. Do you get the point? God isn't playing guessing games with us. We aren't naming tunes, but we should be accurate and definitive when naming the needs in our lives. When we pray specifically about them, we will receive the results we desire. Answered prayer is a good "prize" to be won. Some people pray, "Lord, bless everybody." The Lord can't do much with a prayer like that.

Pray the Word of God

What does it mean to be specific in the way you pray? The most important ingredient in any prayer should be the Word of God—or, at least, the knowledge that what you pray is the will of God. I like to pray the Word back to the Father in Jesus' name. I know God will always honor the promises of His Word when they are prayed in faith.

Pray with Faith

Of course, faith is the next ingredient. The Lord told a noted evangelist not to pray unless he knew that when he prayed, the answer was forthcoming. This man said it drastically abbreviated his prayer life and changed nearly all of it. One time, the Lord told me not to waste His time or mine by praying unbelieving, ineffective prayers.

Get to the Heart of the Matter

Next, get right to the heart of a matter. The kind of prayer you pray is very important. In other words, if someone is demon oppressed, a prayer for healing will not be too effective. You need to bind the demonic activity, and it is of great benefit to deal with the particular kind of oppression involved. When an individual's business is on the verge of bankruptcy, don't just ask the Lord to heal the business. Learn all you can about the specifics that brought the business to this point, and deal with every one of those details when you pray about the matter. If you are praying about a broken relationship in your life, then examine your own heart, settle anything that needs to be settled there, and deal with the obvious things that brought about the problem.

Ask for the Holy Spirit's Help

Ask the Holy Spirit to show you things that may be pertinent to any prayer you pray. One of the most effective prayers I know in this regard was prayed by Paul in Ephesians 1:17. I make it personal every day: "Lord, give me the spirit of wisdom and revelation in the knowledge of Christ." Paul assured us in 1 Corinthians 1:30 that Christ Jesus *"became for us wisdom."* We need the Lord's wisdom to know how to pray and what to pray. That wisdom is promised to us. (See also James 1:5–8.)

> *Every day, you can pray, "Lord, give me the spirit of wisdom and revelation in the knowledge of Christ."*

Paul was a giant in prayer, and the results in his life prove it. This man strongly recommended praying in the Holy Spirit. Do you want to pray the perfect will of God concerning each matter? In Romans 8:27, Paul said that the Holy Spirit intercedes for us according to the will of God. Verse 28 tells us that when we pray the will of God, He is able to work all the things in our lives for good. Pray with the Spirit, and God will turn around that problem for you! In Ephesians 6:18, Paul wrote, *"Praying always with all prayer and supplication in the Spirit."* I'm convinced that praying in tongues, or praying in the Holy Spirit, helps prioritize the needs and issues in your prayer time.

Six Basic Things Jesus Identified as Sickness

Now, I want to look at six basic things that Jesus identified as sickness. In order to obtain the most effective results, we, too, need to identify these things when we pray for healing.

1. Torments

The first general area is "torments." In Matthew 4:24, we read,

> *And they brought to Him [Jesus] all sick people who were afflicted with various diseases and torments, and those who were demon-possessed, epileptics, and paralytics; and He healed them.*

Jesus identified some sicknesses as torments. This kind of torment comes from demonic harassment. It can be mental, emotional, or physical. Mental hospitals and psychiatric clinics are full of people who are tormented mentally and emotionally by demons. These people have unwittingly allowed Satan room in their thought life with such things as fear, insecurity, hurt, offenses, anger, and unforgiveness. Torments also attack the body. Jesus came to heal us of all vexing, tormenting illnesses. With just a word, He healed the centurion's servant who was dreadfully tormented with paralysis.

(See Matthew 8:5–13.) Again, He healed a woman's daughter whose sickness was the result of being *"severely demon-possessed."* (See Matthew 15:22–28.) Jesus was not in the presence of either of the affected people when He healed them. You see, Satan has to bow his knee to the Word of God, no matter what the circumstances.

A venerable missionary, one well acquainted with the ways of the devil, told an interesting account of being tormented by an evil spirit when he was ministering in a foreign land. For a brief period of time, he felt this evil entity trying to attack him through various tormenting things. Then, one night, his bed just started moving across the floor. Having learned how to deal with the devil, the man commanded, "Move the bed back, in Jesus' name!" The missionary said the bed immediately moved back into its previous location.

This same man delivered a young woman jailed for prostitution. While she was imprisoned, terribly painful bites would appear on her body. Both her arms were scarred with the teeth marks of some invisible assailant. Several of the prison officials who tried to deal with the woman died after she put a curse on them. When the missionary read the account in the local paper, God commanded him to go to the prison and deliver the woman. After putting up an argument, he did go and successfully cast the demons out of the woman. She was delivered and healed, accepted Christ, and gave up her life of sin, and she is still serving the Lord today. What a miraculous "healing"!

The devil comes with a variety of torments for the purpose of afflicting you or making you afraid of him. He will torment you with thoughts, fears, and anxieties, all designed to oppress you and make you his slave. Nagging, persistent things are torments. I put allergies under the category of torments. Allergy-ridden people are continually bothered with various symptoms, such as headaches, stuffy noses, and swollen eyes. I think asthma and emphysema are tormenting diseases. Satan's demons come with various kinds of sicknesses, diseases, and infirmities to kill your body; but Jesus came to heal you of all the devil's fiendish torments.

I know a woman who was tormented with allergies all her life. They were becoming more serious all the time; they were sapping her strength and affecting her work. After this person was filled with the Holy Spirit, she really took hold of healing, and miracle after miracle virtually delivered her family from all sickness. However, she was still tormented with the allergies. One day, the Lord shocked the lady to attention with this question: *Why do you still have those allergies?* She pondered the question and thought, *Why, indeed?* Promptly, she applied the healing work of Jesus to the tormenting condition, and within twenty-four hours, every symptom was gone. Occasionally, the devil tries to bring back a symptom, but she rebukes it, and it flees! Sometimes, we hang on to tormenting things because we've become so used to them that they just seem a part of us. Don't let the devil torment you that way. Give it back to him, in Jesus' name!

2. Plagues, or Afflictions

For He healed many, so that as many as had afflictions ["plagues"* KJV] pressed about Him to touch Him.* (Mark 3:10)

The Greek word translated *"afflictions"* or *"plagues"* literally means "whip" or "scourge." The dictionary defines *plague* as "an epidemic disease that causes high mortality." We think of a plague as some dreadful disease that sweeps across a large segment of society, bringing with it death and destruction. In the early 1900s, a virile strain of flu ravaged our nation. Few homes were untouched, and the death rate was staggering. A plague is also referred to as a continuing or long-lasting illness. Jesus said that the woman who had a hemorrhaging condition for many years was sick of a *"plague."* (See Mark 5:34 KJV.)

Polio was a plague that, for years, put fear in the heart of every parent until a vaccine was found to prevent the paralyzing disease. "Childhood" diseases such as chicken pox and measles can be considered plagues. Scarlet fever and typhoid fever still ravage Third World nations, and a plague thought to have been conquered is again raising its ugly head. That plague is tuberculosis. Certainly, cancer is a plague. It touches large numbers of our population from infancy to old age, and it can attack any area of the body. Modern science has made some strides in helping cancer patients, but this dread condition is still a fearsome threat.

There is no question that today we would consider AIDS a plague. In America, this hideous, death-dealing disease began in the homosexual community and spread to the heterosexual segment of our society. It can also be passed through the contaminated needle of a drug user, or from blood transfused from an infected person. Thousands are dying from this disease in the United States each year, while in other nations and continents, such as Africa, AIDS is causing widespread devastation. In 2009, there were 1.8 million AIDS-related deaths in adults and children worldwide (1.3 million of these in sub-Saharan Africa), with over 33 million living with HIV/AIDS (22.5 million in sub-Saharan Africa). There also were an estimated 16.6 million orphans worldwide due to AIDS.[2] If this plague is not stopped, millions more of the world's population will die. Medical science is in a breakneck race with time to find a cure, BUT—I have good news! Jesus is healing people with AIDS. The name of Jesus is greater than any plague you can name.

> *The name of Jesus is greater than any plague you can name.*

In Mark 3:10, we read of Jesus healing many people who were sick with plagues, and verse 11 infers these plagues were the result of *"unclean spirits."* However, these spirits were no match for the Lord. The people were delivered and made whole. The Lord has never left His people helpless in the face of plagues. When God inspired Moses to write

---

[2] http://www.avert.org/worldstats.htm.

the first five books of the Bible, He said the "blood covenant" people who obeyed His commands would be free from *all manner* of sickness and disease. (See Exodus 15:26.) That includes plagues. Born-again believers are blood covenant people, too, and the blood of Jesus Christ will cleanse our blood from any plague.

During the nineteenth century, the highly contagious bubonic plague swept across the continent of Africa, where John G. Lake worked as a missionary. The British government was attempting to inoculate as many people as it could. Everyone who was known to be ill with the disease was quarantined. Without inoculation, Mr. Lake was going into the quarantined areas to pray for the sick, and many were being healed. However, when the officials heard what the missionary was doing, they insisted he stop. In order to prove that he was immune to the plague, Mr. Lake placed in the palm of his hand some froth from the mouth of a dying patient. Microscopic examination proved the multitude of live germs in the froth died on contact with Mr. Lake's hand. Needless to say, he was allowed to continue his ministry among the sick.

Psalm 91:10 contains a wonderful promise for those who will claim it: *"No evil shall befall you, nor shall any plague come near your dwelling."* This psalm contains a treasure of promises, and most of them can be applied to healing. Nothing is too hard for the Lord, but we must meet His conditions: *"He who dwells in the secret place of the Most High shall abide under the shadow of the Almighty"* (verse 1). To abide under that shadow is to have victory over sickness and premature death, *"because you have made the LORD, who is my refuge, even the Most High, your dwelling place"* (verse 9). When Jesus is Lord of your life, you will *"tread upon the lion and the cobra, the young lion and the serpent you shall trample underfoot"* (verse 13). You have power and authority over Satan and all his demons!

3. Oppressions

When God anointed Jesus with the Holy Spirit and power, He went about doing good and *healing* all those who were *oppressed by* the devil. (See Acts 10:38.) I believe oppression begins in the mind when individuals unknowingly accept the deceiver's lies. Really, the only thing the devil can use against people is ignorance and deception. If you are ignorant of God's truth about a matter, Satan can deceive you with his lies. The better acquainted you are with the Word of God, the less able Satan is to deceive you. Jesus said, *"If you abide in My word, you are My disciples indeed.* **And you shall know the truth**, *and the truth shall make you free"* (John 8:31–32).

Unfortunately, many fine Christians have been deceived by denominational doctrine that doesn't agree with the truth of God's Word. Again, how many well-meaning people have you met who are "suffering for Jesus" because they believe this is pleasing to the Lord? These people think their sicknesses or unfortunate circumstances have been allowed or even planned by God to humble or mature them. They grin and bear it but never try to remove it, because they have been told God will reward them according to how patiently they have suffered. This is oppression! No one will ever reach *spiritual* maturity through the affliction of the *flesh*. Such thinking opens the door to whatever the devil may bring your way.

> *Let no one keep defrauding you of your prize by delighting in self-abasement....These are matters which have, to be sure, the appearance of wisdom in self-made religion and self-abasement and severe treatment of the body, but are of no value against fleshly indulgence.*   (Colossians 2:18, 23 NASB)

One time, a lovely young Christian woman came to me for counseling because she was under very dangerous mental oppression. This lady was attractive and happily married with four young children; the family was healthy, and they were serving the Lord. She had "everything going for her," and yet the enemy had begun to whisper a deadly lie to her. She would be going about her household tasks, and this voice would say, *You're going to die. Enjoy life while you can, because you do not have long to live.* Assuming the message came from God, she believed it. As you might guess, she soon went into depression.

Fortunately, the insidious lie was exposed when the lady finally shared it with her husband. When he assured her through the Word that God hadn't authored such thoughts, she realized she had listened to the devil. The truth of God's Word set this woman free from an oppression that surely would have taken her life. She rooted up the lies and transplanted Bible promises into her mind and into her heart. She learned that God had a good future planned for her and would satisfy her with long life. (See Jeremiah 29:11; Psalm 91:16.) She put her thoughts on the Lord, and He brought His peace to her mind. (See Isaiah 26:3.)

The devil will lie to you and try to make you think his lies are from God. Satan may plant these thoughts directly into your mind, or he may use other people to plant thoughts that are contrary to God's will and His Word. In either case, if you begin to entertain Satan's lies, they will become "futile thoughts" (see Romans 1:21), or "vain imaginations" (KJV), and the imaginations will become strongholds. I'm telling you, oppression begins in the mind. Once the enemy gets his lies into the arena of the mind, he is able to put oppressive sickness on the body. The devil knows this very well. That is why he attacks your thought life. Oppression is a hideous thing, but Jesus can set you free from any oppression, whether it's mental or physical. I'm convinced that mental and physical breakdowns are illnesses of oppression. I would also include anxiety attacks and debilitating stress that causes a variety of illnesses, such as spastic colons and ulcers.

> *For though we walk in the flesh, we do not war according to the flesh. For the weapons of our warfare are not carnal but mighty in God for pulling down strongholds, casting down arguments ["imaginations" KJV] and every high thing that exalts itself against the knowledge of God, bringing every thought into captivity to the obedience of Christ.*
> (2 Corinthians 10:3–5)

> *God has given us the authority to bring every thought into submission to the Word of God.*

Notice that the warfare takes place in the mind, but God has given us the authority to cast down devilish arguments, or imaginations, and to bring every thought into submission to the Word of God. Don't allow Satan to establish strongholds in your mind or to put oppression on your body. Cast out every speculation that does not agree with the Word. Use God's Word as the measuring stick for every thought in your mind.

4. Infirmities

Jesus also healed people of "infirmities." Luke 13:11–13 tells of a woman who had been crippled by a *"spirit of infirmity"* for eighteen years. Her body was bent over, and she could not stand upright. When Jesus saw this poor cripple, He called her forward and said, *"Woman, you are loosed from your infirmity"* (verse 12). Then, He laid His hands on her, and immediately the woman stood erect.

Matthew 8:16–17 records an occasion when Jesus healed all the sick in His presence, *"that it might be fulfilled which was spoken by Isaiah the prophet, saying: 'He Himself took our infirmities and bore our sicknesses'"* (verse 17). (See Isaiah 53:4.)

Luke 5:15 tells of multitudes of people who came to Jesus to be healed of their infirmities. In Luke 7:20–22, Jesus proved to John the Baptist's disciples that He was the Messiah by curing many people of infirmities and afflictions, or plagues.

An infirmity is something that causes a person to be "not firm," or lacking in wholeness. A condition that makes an individual weak or feeble is referred to as an infirmity. Debilitating diseases such as muscular dystrophy or multiple sclerosis can be classified as infirmities. Many wheelchair victims suffer from some sort of infirmity. As some people get older, their bodies lose strength, and they become infirm—feeble or tottery. People can become feeble in mind as well as body. Both senility and Alzheimer's disease are infirmities of the mind. The word *infirm* also means "unstable or irresolute in one's thinking and actions."

I heard an amusing but very practical story of a woman who applied Romans 8:26 to gain victory over her weakness, or infirmity—bad eating habits. This Scripture says that when we do not know what to pray, the Spirit comes to our aid and strengthens us in our weaknesses. The lady knew that food was her weakness, so she determined that in her weakness, Jesus would be her strength. (See 2 Corinthians 12:9–10.) Before every meal, she prayed in the Spirit for ten minutes and then found that she was not as hungry as usual. She was able to resist the wrong foods and second helpings. As a result, she got down to her desired weight and felt much better about herself, not just in body but also in soul. She had won over her infirmity.

I have a beautiful testimony about a grandmother and her five-year-old granddaughter. Ever since the child was two years old, she had been afflicted with a terrible infirmity called juvenile arthritis. The disease had crippled the child until she couldn't walk, so her little body was confined to a wheelchair. The grandmother brought this child to one of my meetings, expecting the little girl to be healed. For three days, the grandmother had prepared her heart and her mind for a miracle. She had meditated on God's Word and claimed numerous healing Scriptures. In her mind, she painted a picture of her granddaughter running and playing. This woman purposed in her heart not to leave the meeting until the little girl was healed. That evening during the prayer time, the crippled girl simply got out of the wheelchair and started walking around the room. Jesus had healed this precious child of the infirmity. Praise the Lord!

Infirmities, or weaknesses, are often inherited. We hear of conditions such as diabetes or heart disease being passed down from generation to generation. When a doctor examines you, he asks if there is a history of any diseases in your family. He expects this information to give him clues to your own present physical condition and to aid him in treating you now or in the future. Some insurance companies want to know before they insure you whether there are certain illnesses to which you may be susceptible through heredity. If there are, you are considered a high-risk policyholder.

Although a medical insurer doesn't want to pay a claim for an anticipated illness, the cost of your claiming an inherited infirmity is much greater. Put a stop to such things and tell these sicknesses and infirmities never to appear again in you or any member of your family. You don't have to have the infirmities of your earthly parents or grandparents; God is your heavenly Father, and He is not infirm! Your inheritance is in Christ Jesus, so don't allow the devil to put any of his infirmities on you.

Tell sicknesses and infirmities never to appear again in you or any member of your family.

> Therefore, if anyone is in Christ, he is a new creation; old things have passed away; behold, all things have become new.
> (2 Corinthians 5:17)

5. Bondage

One day in the synagogue, Jesus read aloud Isaiah 61:1–2 and shocked the listeners by saying the prophet's words were fulfilled in Him that day. (See Luke 4:17–21.) Isaiah said the Messiah would *"proclaim liberty to the captives, and the opening of the prison to those who are bound"* (Isaiah 61:1). Later, when Jesus healed the woman who had been bent over for eighteen years by an *"infirmity,"* He said she had been *"bound"* by Satan. This *"daughter of Abraham"* had been in bondage to the devil's evil work, but the Lord loosed her body from the imprisonment that had bound her for so long. (See Luke 13:10–16.) Jesus said sickness holds people in bondage, but He came to set us free.

Anyone who has been sick knows that sickness is a bondage. Acute illness puts you in bed, drains you of strength, and keeps you from your regular activities. With less severe illnesses, you feel like you are just dragging around, not able to function normally. The body is bound by sickness. It's as though you have invisible ropes around you that won't let you go. Someone addicted to a substance such as tobacco, alcohol, or drugs knows what a bondage is, and most addicts are unable to free themselves from such bondage. These substances produce a number of serious, even fatal, conditions in a human body.

Romans 8:15 contains a wonderful nugget of truth more precious than gold: *"For you did not receive the spirit of bondage again to fear, but you received the Spirit of adoption by whom we cry out, 'Abba, Father.'"* Years ago, people subjugated other people in the bondage of institutionalized slavery, but to this day, Satan still holds multitudes in the bondage of sin and sickness. However, there is good news: Christ has freed the slaves! All humanity was bound with chains of sin, sickness, poverty, and death until Jesus bought us out of the slave market of sin at the price of His own precious blood. When we are born again, our heavenly Father adopts us into His family, where there is life, liberty, health, and wealth.

A woman wrote to share an outstanding healing. Her little daughter had hydrocephalus, a condition in which fluid is retained on the brain, causing a distorted enlargement of the head. Usually, the victim is both mentally and physically handicapped by this atrocious affliction. The mother received a prayer cloth from our ministry, and soon after she placed it on her daughter's body, the child's condition began to improve steadily. When the mother wrote to us, her daughter was able to feed herself and comb her hair, and she was beginning to speak. What a terrible bondage, but Jesus gave the victory.

6. Captivity

"To preach deliverance to the captives" (Luke 4:18). We have all heard of Job's suffering, but how many realize the Bible refers to the tragedy and physical affliction that plagued Job as *"captivity"*? *"And the LORD turned the captivity of Job, when he prayed for his friends: also the LORD gave Job twice as much as he had before"* (Job 42:10 KJV).

The story of Job is a perfect example of what Jesus said in John 10:10: *"The thief does not come except to steal, and to kill, and to destroy. I have come that they may have life, and that they may have it more abundantly."* Remembering that Satan was the one who brought the captivity upon Job, we realize that it is the devil who holds us as his captives when he puts sickness upon us. That makes me "fighting mad," and I am determined to free as many people as I can from Satan's prison of sickness and disease.

I want to share with you the thrilling testimony of a woman who was healed of multiple sclerosis. She wrote, "I was finally able to let go of all the fears related to the MS which had kept me a *prisoner* for over 24 years. Thanks to God's love and the sacrifice of my precious Lord Jesus, I'm healed—I'm FREE!"

At the age of sixteen, this lady had been diagnosed with the disease that held her captive for over half her life. Then, one day, she told a friend she was sick and tired of being sick. Her friend began to open the healing Scriptures to her; and, after some time, when the woman was convinced Jesus could heal her, the friend's sister prayed for the woman who had been held so long in Satan's prison.

I quote again from her letter: "When my friend's sister laid hands on me and cast out the MS in the name of Jesus, I felt a warmth all through me. She touched various parts of my afflicted body, and I was a bit scared. Yet I felt a peace and calm when she finished."

The lady saw no immediate improvement, but she kept speaking the Word until she was able to accept her healing as done. From that moment, the woman began to improve, and she became totally free from multiple sclerosis, glory to God!

Some Things May Need to Be Changed

Jesus asked the crippled man beside the pool of Bethesda a specific question. It was, *"Do you want to be made well ["whole"* KJV]?" (John 5:6). Now I ask you the same question: "Do you want to be whole?" Who in the world would not answer in the affirmative? The man to whom the Lord spoke had been trying for thirty-eight years to get into that pool ahead of anyone else, because he believed he'd be healed if he did so. This man's thinking didn't go beyond his crippled body, but Jesus knew the man needed a *total healing* in his spirit, his soul, and his body. Therefore, he asked the man if he wanted to be made complete and perfect in his entire being.

Remember that Jesus healed the man with just a command: *"Rise, take up your bed and walk"* (verse 8). When Jesus encountered the man later, in the temple, He told him, *"See, you have been made well. Sin no more, **lest a worse thing come upon you"*** (verse 14). The emphasis is mine, but I truly believe this is where Jesus put the emphasis. Healing comes from the inside out; apparently, this man's sinful ways had opened the door to Satan's vicious attack on his body. The Lord warned the man that his attitude and his behavior would determine whether he would stay well. The message of John the Baptist was, *"Repent, for the kingdom of heaven is at hand!"* (Matthew 3:2). Obviously, repentance opened the door for the blessings of God. This meant restoration of every kind, including healing.

> *Repentance opened the door for the blessings of God. This meant restoration of every kind, including healing.*

The Greek word for *"repent"* is *metanoeo*, which means "to change one's mind and go in a different direction." Jesus knows that when people change their minds about sin, He can change the direction of their lives. When attitudes and emotions are changed toward godliness, motives and actions become holy, and lives are made whole.

Ideas That Can Hinder Healing

Many times, when my mind has not been wholly in line with God's Word, I have not received healing until I've repented and agreed with the truth. When I get my mind in line with the Word, my body gets in line with the Word. Let me tell you about some ideas that can hinder or prevent your physical healing.

"The World Owes Me Happiness"

Give up the idea that the world owes you happiness. People are so prone to think they deserve whatever it is they want. Folks, the world does not owe you happiness, and there is nothing any of us deserves, outside of Jesus Christ, except judgment. Remember that. There are people who are never satisfied with anything. If they eat in a fine restaurant, they will not enjoy the food; if it's a beautiful day, they remind you that the weather will probably change. If you mention how nice someone looks, they will find something about that person's appearance they don't like. This kind of negativity is deadly.

> But know this, that in the last days perilous times will come: for men will be lovers of themselves,...lovers of pleasure rather than lovers of God. (2 Timothy 3:1–2, 4)

In America, we have the "gimmes"; our society is geared that way. Advertising is planned to feed the gimmes from the cradle to the grave. Of course, you understand the gimmes—give me this and give me that. The more we get, the more we want—and the more discontent we are. However, if we will quit demanding for ourselves and start giving to others out of pure, selfless motives, then we will discover happiness and contentment. When we start counting our blessings and looking for the good things in life and in others, we will find satisfaction. *What an environment that is for healing!* I believe our nation can be healed when we, the people, start looking to God instead of to self and our own pursuit of happiness.

"I Deserve to Feel This Way"

Give up the idea that you can harbor fear, resentment, bitterness, unforgiveness, anger, and guilt. This is all self-centeredness. Don't think you will continue to enjoy health and healing with this kind of attitude. Thinking like this pours poison into the human system, and negative thoughts are self-destructive. Wrong thinking is sin, and it will demand an awful payment. No one can be warped in his or her thought life and not become warped in body. Jesus brought salvation to the woman caught in adultery and said, *"Go and sin no more"* (John 8:11). When He healed the man at the pool of Bethesda, He spoke virtually the same message to him: *"Sin no more"* (John 5:14).

Once, I happened to see a talk-show host interviewing four sisters. The topic was what to do when you can't forgive someone who has done something "unforgivable." One sister was deeply embittered toward the other because it had been that sister's boyfriend who had murdered their mother. The unforgiving sister blamed the other sister for her mother's death, because she had dated a person who was known to be violent. When the one sister had quit dating this man, he had killed their mother to "get even." The other two sisters had forgiven the "offending" one, saying that if she had ever needed their love, she needed it now, and if their mother were living, she would forgive and try to reconcile her daughters.

Although I don't know whether the counselor was a Christian, he certainly gave godly counsel to the unforgiving sister. He told her that she must separate the man who committed the crime from the crime itself. The crime was terrible and wrong, but she needed to forgive both the man and her sister, or it would destroy her. He was right on the mark—the young woman was suffering from cancer. What an illustration of how oppression that captivates the mind will also captivate the body! At the end of the show, the TV audience was told that the program had been taped two months earlier. In the meantime, the counselor had spent several hours with the four sisters, and the embittered one had come to genuine forgiveness. I like happy endings. I believe the cancer that had laid hold of that young would have to release her because she released her sister.

"My Healing Must Come Immediately"

Also, give up the idea that every healing must be instantaneous. You must exercise your faith for healing at the time you receive prayer, but the manifestation of the healing may come sometime later. Healing may also be gradual. Yet, in either case, don't abandon your faith. Faith in God's promises will produce the object of your hope. Faith believes for those things that can be seen only in the spirit realm. Your answers eventually will come into view when you continue to believe what you can see

> *Faith in God's promises will produce the object of your hope.*

only in the Word of God. You do not know all the things God must move into place before healing can happen. For example, I don't believe that the unforgiving sister could have been healed of cancer or maintained her healing until her mind and attitude had been healed. When Jesus does a work, He desires to do a complete work.

Healing may be manifested sometime after a person receives prayer. However, the more determined a person is to experience healing, the more faith is exercised, and the less likely it is that the individual will ever lose the healing. Keep in mind that as far as God is concerned, the matter is finished, and He is working out the details. Many people come to me days, weeks, and even months after prayer to report their healings. A woman in our church had a growth on her scalp, so she stood for prayer when I was cursing growths, tumors, and warts. She saw absolutely no change in the disturbing growth, but every time her comb accidentally scraped it, she thanked God she was healed. Six months later, she reached up to scratch her head, and the thing fell off in her hand.

"I'll Skip the Spiritual Healing and Just Take Physical Healing"

Give up the idea that you can skip spiritual healing and just take physical healing. Once, on a trip to Russia, we saw dozens of people miraculously healed. One Russian woman who had seen many of these healings occur came to the platform and said, "I see you believe in healing the sick. I'm a white witch, and I can teach you some new ways to produce healing." Folks, I don't care if they are white witches or witches of any other color, I'm not interested, no matter "witch" way they believe! These people believe they are doing good, but they are tools of the devil. Again, Satan has supernatural power, and he may counterfeit healing; but he is in the business of ensnaring souls, not freeing them.

This "white" witch was interested only in people's bodies; but Jesus is interested in the spirit, the soul, and the body. He wants to heal the whole person. Don't think that you can deal with symptoms without getting to the root of an illness. Many times, we look at some outward symptom and try to get that healed when there is some underlying problem that needs attention. If there is, the sick person will never enjoy healing and health until the entire issue is brought to light. The Holy Spirit will lead us into all truth; so, no matter what the problem, He can show it to us, and the appropriate prayer can be prayed. It is so important that we pray effectively in order for the sick person to receive not only complete healing but also healing that lasts.

For example, people who have had all kinds of prayer for incessant indigestion and heartburn may not be healed until they change their eating habits. Others with foot problems may have to lose weight, and I've seen people healed in their bodies when they had infected teeth pulled. One of our staff members had painful blisters appear on her toes. After she prayed, the Lord showed her the condition wasn't athlete's foot or some horrible dermatitis. All she had to do was remove her nylons before putting on sport socks and tennis shoes when she walked during her lunch period. When she did, the blisters soon disappeared. Even though this person was trying to improve her health through exercise, she was unknowingly chafing her feet.

How to Stay Well

The following are two important keys to staying well that will counteract the ideas that hinder healing.

Walk in Love

First, anything in your thought life, your attitudes, or your actions that isn't in accord with love must *go*. If you are nursing some hurt or unforgiveness, let it go. If you play unclean fantasies on the screen of your mind, let them go. If you avoid some relative or neighbor because you've been offended, clear the air and let it go. You must walk in love. Not only did Jesus command us to do so, but a love walk is also necessary to stay whole and healthy. The Lord doesn't want unloving thoughts or actions to prevent you from walking in health. Love has correction in it.

Loving parents correct their children because they care about them, and our heavenly Father corrects His children because He loves them and wants them to enjoy the benefits of health. First Corinthians 13 is a wonderful recipe for love.

Let Go of All "Crutches"

The next way to stay in health is to let go of all the "crutches." Examine your thinking. Do you sometimes enjoy being sick, or do you believe you have a right to feel the way you do? I heard a minister say that his mother didn't want to be healed of crippling arthritis because she felt she had a right to all the help and attention she received as a result of the condition. She had waited on her children while they were growing up, and she thought it was their turn to wait on her. And she had taken care of her husband's needs for years, so she thought it was time he took care of her needs.

You gave up your "rights" when you came to Jesus. You gave up *your* rights, but you received all of *His* rights. In Christ, you have the right to be healed, you have the right to walk in divine health, and you have the right to be whole in every area of your life. Be careful about those crutches that rob you of God's expectations. Don't expect to be sick because you are overworked; don't expect to get the flu when everyone

> *Expect to be healed and to stay healed, because that is the will of God.*

else does. Expect to *be* healed and to *stay* healed, because that is the will of God. Put God's thoughts in your mind, and remember this:

> *But if the Spirit of him that raised up Jesus from the dead dwell in you, he that raised up Christ from the dead shall also quicken your mortal bodies by his Spirit that dwelleth in you.* (Romans 8:11 KJV)

10

God's Dinner Bell Is Ringing

G od's supernatural touch in the life of a Christian is His "dinner bell" to the world; it rings out the invitation, "Come and dine." (See Isaiah 55:1–3.) Yes, it is a blessing to the one who receives it, but it also affords that person the opportunity to be an undeniable testimony to the unbeliever. The world should see every one of us walking in divine health, divine prosperity, and divine power and authority. It would be impossible for me to count the times I've seen miraculous healings open the door of people's hearts; and they, too, have stepped into the kingdom to sit and to sup with Jesus and to taste the good things He has for them. (See Revelation 3:20.)

I'm thinking now of a woman who "sowed" a godly life before her unsaved husband. Miracles in her life had repeatedly rung the dinner bell, but the chimes had fallen on deaf ears. Years went by, and she had plenty of time to either give up or keep on sowing precious seeds for an even bigger harvest. Then, this man was stricken with a serious heart attack. Of course, the devil would like to have taken him out of the game before he reached "home." But do you know that God and His team are better at playing the game of life than the devil and his team are at playing the game of death?

This unbelieving husband was touched by the miraculous power of God in such a dramatic way that just a few days after the heart attack, the doctors were scratching their heads in wonder. Every test showed the man had a normal heart, as though he had never had a heart attack. Isn't that just like the Lord? In this case, God performed the healing on the unbeliever himself. The heart attack brought the man to attention, and the miracle he experienced in his own body finally caused him to give his attention to the gospel. He couldn't deny his own healing, and he knew Jesus Christ had a claim on his life. The wife not only saw her husband's physical heart healed, but she also saw his spirit touched by the power of God.

The ringing of God's dinner bell can be heard all over the earth. God does not show partiality; Jesus died for the whole world. (See Acts 10:34–35.) God's table is set for every kindred and every tribe (see Revelation 5:9), and they are coming by the thousands to His banquet. On one of my missions trips to Russia, my ministry team and I saw thousands respond to God's dinner bell as we witnessed miracle after miracle of healing. The anointing was so heavy that all the members of the team saw people healed as the team prayed for them.

After one of the meetings, a team member had just stepped outside the building when a Russian lady shoved her daughter in front of her. This lady had heard the dinner bell, and she was determined that her child would hear it, too. Although there was a language barrier, the mother was able to show the woman that her child was deaf. The woman prayed, and instantly the little girl's ears were opened—she could hear! One woman on our team was healed of terrible varicose veins in her legs after three other team members prayed for her. This woman, who spoke fluent Russian, received her miracle at a time when she was "feeding" the Word of God to a group of hungry Russians. Again, the dinner bell rang.

God orchestrated another miraculous situation on this trip to Russia. One man and his wife went with gifts and money for a Russian couple they had never met. Friends of theirs had loaded them with the gifts for the husband and wife. The two Russians traveled nine hundred miles to Moscow, where we were, to receive the gifts from America. The husband and wife were a captive audience in our meeting, and they both accepted Jesus as their Savior and Lord. These precious people received the greatest healing of all, the healing of their souls. I share this story to illustrate how infinitely God cares for all of us. Now, this Russian family has the gift of salvation to share with their friends, and the gift just keeps on giving.

Every good gift and every perfect gift is from above, and comes down from the Father of lights, with whom there is no variation or shadow of turning. (James 1:17)

Every one of us in Christ has received the power to be like our heavenly Father. Since there is no change in Him, there should be no change in us, except to be continually changing into a more perfect likeness of Jesus:

But we all, with unveiled face, beholding as in a mirror the glory of the Lord, are being transformed into the same image from glory to glory, just as by the Spirit of the Lord.

(2 Corinthians 3:18)

> *In the fullness of His humanity, Christ demonstrated that we can continually walk in victory and health through the power of the Holy Spirit.*

When we step on the rung of God's ladder marked "healing," the next step we take should be a step up to "health." You'll never progress upward if you take a step backward.

When we have received a healing, it is never God's intention for us to lose it. In the fullness of Christ's humanity, He demonstrated to us that we can continually walk in victory and health through the power of the Holy Spirit. Even though Jesus was tempted in every way we will ever be tempted (see Hebrews 2:1; 4:15–16), His earthly life was continual proof that we, too, can live constantly in the life of God. We don't have to be well today and sick tomorrow. We can be unchanging in the power of God's divine life.

Three Unique Aspects of God's Healing Power

Look with me at three things that are unique about God's healing power.

Geographical Location Cannot Hinder It

First, geographical location can't hinder the power of God to heal. Again, when Jesus healed the centurion's servant, the servant wasn't there with Him. Jesus spoke the word, and the servant was healed. When Jesus spoke a word in Israel, a woman's daughter was healed in Phoenicia. Earlier, we looked at Psalm 107:20, which says that God sends His Word to heal. Every time we pray a healing prayer for someone who is not with us, the Word is being sent to heal. I might add that God's power to heal is not stronger in one place than it is in another, simply because of location. We tend to think everything is better in America, but I want to tell you that more people are being healed today in Third World nations than in the United States.

Jesus Always Knows the Outcome

Next, Jesus always knows the end from the beginning; He knows the outcome of every illness. Jesus didn't rush down to Bethany when He received news of Lazarus' critical illness. He waited in Jerusalem until He knew by the Holy Spirit that Lazarus was no longer ill but dead. This was a heartbreaking situation for Mary and Martha, but Jesus knew they soon would be rejoicing over a greater miracle than healing. Jesus raised their brother from the dead! (See John 11:1–45.) If we stay in God's Word until we are convinced of His promises, we don't have to get rattled and nervous about the end result of a difficult matter. We can know that God intends to bring healing and victory every time. That is always His purpose, and He has the power to bring it to pass for those who are trusting in Him.

Jesus' Healing Is Complete

The third unique thing about the Lord's healing is that it is complete. He doesn't do a halfway job. However, we sometimes receive healing for one thing in our bodies, while another physical problem seems to drag on endlessly. In some cases, it seems much easier to believe for the healing of "little" things, while "bigger" things seem beyond the reach of our faith. That is not the way the Lord wants it to be. In His earthly ministry, He made people whole; He didn't leave them partially well or well in one part of their bodies and sick in another part.

Jesus Still Heals Today

Even though there is a common notion in "parts" of the body of Christ that Jesus does not heal today, the Lord is still healing multitudes of people all around them. If human bodies were made completely whole by Jesus' touch, I'm certain that God doesn't want some of Christ's body well and some of His body sick. It is a tragic irony that there are "parts" of our

Lord's body that remain in sickness because of ig. rance and unbelief. The Lord Jesus wants to touc all believers and make them completely well.

Healing didn't die out with the apostles, as some believe. Note that many people who were healed in the New Testament were not healed by the apostles. Stephen and Philip, who were both deacons, performed great wonders and miracles among the people. (See Acts 6:8; 8:6–7.) A man in Damascus laid hands on Paul, and he regained his sight. (See Acts 9:10–19.) Remember also that Paul—who was not one of the original twelve apostles—healed numerous people, and he did not begin to heal until after Jesus had ascended to heaven. (See, for example, Acts 28:8–9.)

Peter declared that our healing was purchased by the stripes (wounds) that Jesus took upon Himself at Calvary. (See 1 Peter 2:24.) The finished work of Calvary stands forever; and if Jesus is the same yesterday, today, and forever, then you and I can still be healed by those stripes!

The finished work of Calvary stands forever, and we can still be healed by Jesus' stripes!

What Prevents Americans from Being Healed

I next want to examine some things that are keeping Americans from being healed or that cost us our healing after we have received it. Remember, God

Lord's body that remain in sickness because of ignorance and unbelief. The Lord Jesus wants to touch all believers and make them completely well.

Healing didn't die out with the apostles, as some believe. Note that many people who were healed in the New Testament were not healed by the apostles. Stephen and Philip, who were both deacons, performed great wonders and miracles among the people. (See Acts 6:8; 8:6–7.) A man in Damascus laid hands on Paul, and he regained his sight. (See Acts 9:10–19.) Remember also that Paul—who was not one of the original twelve apostles—healed numerous people, and he did not begin to heal until after Jesus had ascended to heaven. (See, for example, Acts 28:8–9.)

Peter declared that our healing was purchased by the stripes (wounds) that Jesus took upon Himself at Calvary. (See 1 Peter 2:24.) The finished work of Calvary stands forever; and if Jesus is the same yesterday, today, and forever, then you and I can still be healed by those stripes!

The finished work of Calvary stands forever, and we can still be healed by Jesus' stripes!

What Prevents Americans from Being Healed

I next want to examine some things that are keeping Americans from being healed or that cost us our healing after we have received it. Remember, God not only wants us to get it, but He also wants us to *keep* it! I'm going to deal strictly with those who live in America, because our whole society is being hurt and damaged by wrong thoughts, attitudes, and actions. I call this condition "American paganism." Pagans are irreligious or hedonistic (self-indulgent to the extreme) people. In general, Americans "do their own thing"; if it feels good, we do it—whether or not it hurts anyone else. Praise the Lord, we still have some "salty" Christians who are preserving our nation.

> *A sound heart is life to the body....Wisdom rests in the heart of him who has understanding, but what is in the heart of fools is made known. Righteousness exalts a nation, but sin is a reproach to any people.*
> (Proverbs 14:30, 33–34)

The "Eat, Drink, and Be Merry, for Tomorrow We Die" Attitude

There is the attitude in our culture that you are young only once, so live it up BIG. It's the hopeless philosophy of the "eat, drink, and be merry, for tomorrow we die" crowd. (See Ecclesiastes 8:15.) Our highways have become "slaughterhouses" for the drunk driver. Americans spend billions of dollars on junk food. And tens of millions of people "play" on the Lord's Day instead of worshipping in His house.

Now, I want to bring this closer to home. Almost without realizing it, we Christians also are permeated with these attitudes. What about the quantities of junk food, carbonated drinks, and empty calories we consume? Or what about the "sipping saints"? Do we think that if it tastes good, we can put it in our bodies without paying the consequences? Christian bodies are not immune to sickness. What about the types of TV programs and movies we watch, or the books and magazines we read? What are you looking at on the Internet? Let me tell you, folks, if only junk goes in, only junk will come out. Let's feast on life and not on death! We receive only one body in which to live this life, and a body used for self-indulgence will surely not be full of health.

The Desire for Instant Gratification

Another attitude that has invaded American thought is that we must have instant gratification. We can't wait for anything. We want instant service, instant potatoes, instant coffee, and instant credit. We have drive-through windows at fast-food restaurants and banks, we have express lanes at the supermarket, and we have microwave ovens to heat our "prepared" foods. The list of our "modern conveniences" is endless, but we hardly think about it as we sail through life in the fast lane. Isn't all of this what we deserve?

Let's take a closer look at our "instant" society. Our nation is trillions of dollars in debt, a number of our politicians have been involved in various scandals, banks are going under, all manner of businesses are going bankrupt, and charge cards have plunged multitudes into incredible debt. And we are slaughtering the unborn, who are our the future of our nation. Where is instant gratification taking us? I know we are not all living this way, and I certainly enjoy my modern conveniences; but the attitude that we must have everything we want at the moment we want it is thoughtless and foolish. It leads to heartache and failure; it leads to sickness and death, as we disregard the lives of others, overstress ourselves, and don't take proper care of our bodies, minds, and spirits.

The "Victim Complex"

Americans also have a bad habit of blaming someone or something else for every problem. We take no personal responsibility for our problems. It is always the fault of someone else. America has a "victim" complex. "I wouldn't be sick if this hadn't happened," or "I wouldn't have these problems if I had been loved as a child," or "I grew up in a poor home, my parents were divorced, and my teachers didn't understand me." Secular psychology and psychiatry feed these attitudes, but they don't often present positive solutions. Some lawyers encourage greedy people to sue for every possible cause—real or imagined—so their clients can get what they "deserve" and the lawyers can line their own pockets.

Do you know where all this began? It began with the fall of humanity in the garden of Eden. Adam blamed God for giving him Eve, and Eve blamed the serpent for deceiving her; but God held both Adam and Eve accountable for their sin problem. I realize that many people are damaged by the things that have happened to them, and my heart aches for hurting people. However, there is only one way out of the hurt and the pain. People must stop placing blame, accept responsibility for their lives and their futures, and give the past to Jesus. He is the Healer—the only One who can truly heal our minds, our emotions, and our bodies.

A Dismissal of Everything That Is Beyond Our Understanding

Another mark of American paganism is our insistence upon everything being logical to the human mind. We have become so intellectual that if we can't understand something, we won't believe it. When it isn't in the realm of the natural, where we can hear it, see it, smell it, feel it, or taste it, we simply refuse to believe. If it isn't explainable, we toss it out. This is ridiculous. If we wait to figure out everything, we are going to wait a long time. We are going to miss God, and we are going to miss miracles. Don't miss your miracle of healing because you don't understand how God does it.

How many doctors can explain the essence of life because they know the parts of the human body and how they function? Nevertheless, we still go to doctors. How many astronomers can explain what holds the world in place because they can chart the galaxies? However, the exact precision of the universe is miraculous! Can the evolutionist tell you the origin of that first enzyme or slime that he thinks began the process of life? Do theologians understand everything in the Bible? Of course not. Neither do you nor I; but I accept it as truth, enjoy its blessings, and daily expect the Lord to open my spiritual eyes to greater revelation of the truths in His living Book.

There is no mortal, no matter what his genius, who can begin to figure out the mind and ways of God. Even the least of God's thoughts are greater than any human thought or imagination, *"Because the foolishness of God is wiser than men, and the weakness of God is stronger than men"* (1 Corinthians 1:25). We know that God is never foolish or weak; but with this impossible comparison, we should see that His wisdom and power immeasurably transcend any human thought or strength. In spite of this fact, the Lord promises to put His wisdom and power to work on our behalf *"immeasurably more than all we ask or imagine"* (Ephesians 3:20 NIV).

When we place our trust and confidence in the Lord, He is able to lift us from the natural into the supernatural with one touch of His miraculous power. What difference does it make if we can't understand the operations of God? We can still enjoy all His benefits. The miracle of healing is one of those benefits. God has put into the human body the natural ability to heal itself of many sicknesses, so even without a supernatural miracle, your body is a miracle healing machine. Don't abuse it.

> *When we place our trust in the Lord, He is able to lift us from the natural into the supernatural with one touch of His miraculous power.*

Let the wicked forsake his way, and the unrighteous man his thoughts; let him return

to the LORD, and He will have mercy on
him; and to our God, for He will abundantly pardon. "For My thoughts are not your
thoughts, nor are your ways My ways,"
says the LORD. "For as the heavens are higher than the earth, so are My ways higher
than your ways, and My thoughts than your
thoughts." (Isaiah 55:7–9)

If we try to figure out everything, it is going to get
us out of faith. I can't explain miracles; but when I need
one, all that matters is whether I can receive it. I can't
afford to lose faith; that is far worse than "losing face."
There is no one who can explain how cancers disappear, discs are replaced in spines, or arms and legs are
lengthened. No one can explain how a drug addict or
an alcoholic is set free in an instant from those horrible
bondages. Nevertheless, anyone who has ever received
such a miracle doesn't question that it happened.

Once, I called upon a young man in our congregation to report the healing of his knees. I didn't
ask him to tell the congregation how the miracle happened—I just asked him to share his testimony, and
we all rejoiced with him. Now he could walk without
pain and do many things he couldn't do before. This
man didn't know how God had healed his knees; he
just appreciated and enjoyed the benefits. During this
time, I was teaching a series on healing in our church,
and we saw miracle after miracle. I can't explain how
eyes, ears, and backs were healed; I can't explain how
tumors and warts vanished; but they did. Years ago,
my back was healed when an evangelist prayed for
me. One of my arms was longer than the other, but,

when he prayed, my outstretched arms became the same length before my eyes, and I've never had the back problem since. It was an unexplainable miracle.

What Is Causing Americans to Be Sick

We've looked at some attitudes and actions that prevent Americans from being healed. Now, it is time to look more closely at some of the things that produce sickness in Americans and keep them that way.

Prepared Foods

One of the things that is making Americans sick is our "supermarket diet"—a diet that is full of prepared foods. Nutritionists warn us not to eat the contents of a package if we can't pronounce the ingredients on the label. Much of what we take from the supermarket shelf is either preserved, dyed, or processed. Some of this stuff, even bugs won't eat. Why do we? Not even in the produce section are we safe; the fruits and vegetables have been grown in deficient soil and sprayed with pesticides. When the produce is picked, it is often dyed or waxed; and then, to add insult to injury, the grocer puts it under special lights to make it look fresh and wonderful.

Fat, Sugar, and Junk Food

As if this isn't bad enough, most Americans eat far too much fat, sugar, and junk food. Look into your neighbor's grocery cart when you are standing in the checkout line. For that matter, look into your own. What do you see? Candy, soda pop, baked goods, chips, dips, TV dinners, and the like. Americans are living off the "fat of the land"; and, as a result, they are suffering and dying from high blood pressure, heart disease, cancer, diabetes, and joint problems.

Lack of Exercise

What about exercise—are we burning any of these fat calories? Most of us sit all day in an office, ride in a car everywhere we go, and come home to eat and sit in front of the TV all evening. At least thirty minutes of exercise most days of the week is recommended by health professionals.

Alcohol and Drug Abuse

Then, there is all the alcohol abuse that is destroying lives. Alcohol can lead to impaired mental functions and destroy the liver, the kidneys, and the heart. In short, it can destroy the body. Liquor destroys on the highway, and it destroys in the home. How tragic that so many people think they cannot have a good time or "fit in" with the socially elite without liquor. This liquid drug has captured thousands in the clutches of addiction. I could also mention the devastation that other drugs are causing in our society.

Sexual Promiscuity

If what we Americans eat and drink isn't bad enough, what we do is just as bad. The "sexual revolution" and its legacies have brought sexually transmitted diseases that are running rampant across our nation. I don't know of any revolution that hasn't claimed lives, do you? The new morality is simply old sin, and *"the wages of sin is death"* (Romans 6:23).

Stress

Those of us not sexually promiscuous are not guiltless when it comes to damaging our bodies. We put ourselves under immense stress "keeping up with the Joneses," making our fortunes, pursuing careers, worrying, and doing whatever else we do to put stress on ourselves. This leads to the next point, which is nonstop work.

Workaholism

We are a society of workaholics; it's work, work, work, work. While many people "burn the candle at both ends," they are burning up their bodies, as well.

> *Eating right, drinking plenty of water, getting enough rest, and exercising regularly make any people "lean and mean."*

In contrast, consider the second generation of Israelites who entered the Promised Land. They were born in the wilderness and couldn't push a cart around a supermarket. Their diet was manna for breakfast, manna for lunch, and manna for dinner. God provided them with very healthy food, and He provided refreshing water that gushed from the rock. Those Israelites also got plenty of exercise.

They *walked* everywhere they went; for forty years they walked—from Egypt to the outskirts of Canaan and then all around the desert. When they finally entered the land of promise, they were "lean and mean," well able for the job ahead of them. Eating right, drinking plenty of water, getting enough rest, and exercising regularly make any people "lean and mean." However, when you walk down the streets of America today, you don't see the "lean and mean"; you see the fat and lazy.

The above are some of the major things we Americans are doing that hurt and damage us physically. We all want to be well, but we also want to do our own thing. People who are sick come for healing prayer, and they receive their miracles. Then, many of them go right out and continue to eat improperly, abuse alcohol, or mistreat their bodies in some other way and expect to keep their healings. It simply won't work that way. Everyone, without exception, will reap the consequences of his or her lifestyle. When the rules of good health are broken, the Lord is under no obligation to restore or maintain health in the one who abuses the body.

Although it is always God's pleasure to heal people, we see instances in the Bible when God did not heal. Let's review these occasions and determine why healing was withheld so that we can better understand the principles of healing and health for our own lives.

Earlier in this book, we looked at the case of King Jeroboam's sick son. Jeroboam knew he was in trouble with the Lord, but he still hoped that the

266 TOTAL HEALING

prophet Ahijah would have a good word from God. However, this was not the case, and the boy died. (See 1 Kings 14:1–13.) There was at least one reason why the Lord withheld His healing hand. As we discussed, He saw something good in the child. God did not want this youngster to grow up in an evil, idolatrous environment and become like his father. God's love spared the child from such a fate. Don't forget that the Lord took the boy to a far *better* eternal existence. What was the cost of the king's sin? It was the life of one of his sons, the loss of the throne for his descendants, and essentially the end of the northern tribes of Israel as a kingdom. (See verses 14–16.)

We also noted the death of King David's son, who was born of David's adulterous relationship with Bathsheba. This man cheated and murdered because of his fleshly appetites, but it cost him the life of the little prince. You see, not even kings can break God's rules without paying the consequences. Sin is sin wherever it is found, and it opens the door to satanic attack. Yet David didn't get bitter with God; instead, he got better. He found comfort in the knowledge that he would see his innocent son again in paradise, in spite of his sin. (See 2 Samuel 12:23.) Because of David's deep repentance, another son born of Bathsheba became king after him. Solomon was that son, and he ruled Israel at the pinnacle of its history.

Last, we look at the case of Gehazi, the servant of Elisha. This man served his master well until he was tempted by Naaman's riches. After Naaman was healed of leprosy, he wanted to reward Elisha with money and costly apparel. Elisha refused the Syrian general's gift because it was God who had healed

him. Gehazi, however, just couldn't let this opportunity get away. He followed Naaman, thinking that
Elisha would never know. Gehazi lied to Naaman,
telling him that Elisha had changed his mind about
the gift, and Naaman gave Gehazi some of the silver
and clothing. To Gehazi's dismay, God showed the
prophet what his servant had done. What did Gehazi
pay for his stolen riches? He paid with his health.
The leprosy of Naaman came upon his own body,
and the Scriptures don't say that Gehazi repented or
that he was ever healed. (See 2 Kings 5:20–27.)

A Recipe for Good Health

The above are sobering facts. Every action has
a corresponding reaction. We cannot sin and abuse
our bodies without experiencing the consequences.
Just because we feel well and seem to be in good
health now doesn't mean we are going to stay that
way. If we indulge our appetites, we will pay the
price; and it won't be just at the cash register. Before
you throw up your hands in despair, I want to give
you a recipe you can follow to ensure good health. It
isn't impossible—if you commit yourselfs to God and
a good lifestyle.

The cause of eating right is not hopeless, nor
is it cost prohibitive. You will spend more on junk
food than you will on nutritious foods. Start reading
labels, and eat lots of whole grains, fresh fruits, and
vegetables. You can buy produce that is organically
grown. Prepare meals from scratch and eliminate as
much fat, sugar, and salt from your diet as possible.
Reach for the water glass instead of the pop can or

the beer can; water is the healthiest, most cleansing liquid you can drink.

Don't groan when I mention exercise. Remember, the Bible says that bodily exercise is profitable. (See 1 Timothy 4:8.) Now, it does say that exercise profits for only a little while, but your doctor will tell you the same thing. People can't expect to stay fit if they exercise only once in a while. I don't think any of us eats just one meal a week or sleeps only one night a week. Exercise is a necessity for good health. Any fitness program should include a reasonable amount of exercise. You don't need expensive equipment; walking is one of the very best exercises there is, and most of us have two legs. In years past, people got all the exercise they needed with physical labor, and they walked nearly every place they went.

What about rest? I don't believe it is impossible for the average American to get a sufficient amount of rest. God knows rest is necessary to maintain a healthy body. In every week, the Lord provided one day of rest for His people. Exodus 23:12 says, *"Six days you shall do your work, and on the seventh day you shall rest, that your ox and your donkey may rest, and the son of your female servant and the stranger may be refreshed."*

In spite of a very busy schedule, I find time to rest. Almost without exception, I am able to nap on a daily basis. If I work later than usual at the office, I have a little hideaway where I can lie down on the divan and nap. When I am flying to a Bible Encounter, I nap on the plane. During each Encounter, I find time every day to nap. If I'm overseas, I don't forget my nap. I've napped in airports and on planes, trains, and helicopters. I can nap anyplace, even on the floor. Do you think I'm a baby? Well, I've learned that in order to keep the pace I do and stay refreshed and alert to minister to people, I must include rest in my schedule. I don't believe your body is any different from mine.

If you consistently experience sleepless nights, the devil is robbing you of something that God guarantees. (See Proverbs 3:21–24.) Sleepless nights can be the result of eating the wrong thing or eating too close to bedtime, or of a fearful, angry, or fretful attitude. Memorize Scriptures, meditate on the Word, and pray during those sleepless periods, and cast all of your care on God. When you meditate on God's Word, the Word will lead you, keep you, and speak to you during your waking and sleeping moments. (See Proverbs 6:22.)

Next, how do we cope with stress? Stress is an awful thing. And although we may eliminate some things from our schedules, we all have some stress in our lives. Just normal daily routine puts some stress on our bodies and on our minds. If you are a workaholic, examine the things that are driving you to overwork. You must choose those activities in your schedule that have real, meaningful value and eliminate those things that don't. You don't need to be busy all the time to find self-worth. What will you have in the end if you kill yourself with work?

God has an answer for stress, too. Daily Bible reading and prayer will put your life into the proper perspective and help relieve stress. There is nothing

Bible reading and prayer will put your life into the proper perspective and help relieve stress.

like time spent with the Lord to put your mind and body at ease. Remember that you have a God who loves you enough to order your days. If you are a Spirit-filled Christian, you have the indwelling Holy Spirit who empowers you. He is also with you to guide and comfort you. Learn to rely on Him. The Lord has also given you approximately seven thousand Bible promises to help you through your day. Don't stress yourself with worry and fear; trust God. There is no better recipe for coping with stress.

Now, let's deal with the matter of sex. Many Americans think they are practicing "safe" sex, but the only safe sex is celibacy before marriage and fidelity in marriage. Any other sex is simply illicit, and the person who practices this type of lifestyle is bascially playing Russian roulette. The titillating little office affair, or any other affair, will cost the partners more than they bargained for. I am so grieved that our teenagers are being taught that it's okay if it's "safe." Today, the gay community is anything but gay. Homosexuals are dying from AIDS and many are infected with HIV, and yet many refuse to admit their perversion is sin. God loves these people, but they have opened their bodies to those things that God warns about. (See, for example, Romans 1:20–27.)

Some people who believe in God's miraculous, supernatural power to heal the sick have the notion that it is wrong to go to a doctor. I don't see that idea anywhere in the Bible. In Matthew 9:12, Jesus said, *"Those who are well have no need of a physician, but those who are sick."* In other words, if you are sick, you may need a doctor. The beloved physician Luke was often a companion of Paul's, but I don't find anywhere that Paul rebuked him because of his earlier occupation. There is nothing evil about having periodic checkups or seeing a physician when you are ill. Will seeing the doctor or taking the medication he or she prescribes keep you from being healed if you are trusting God? Go to the doctor and get a diagnosis of your illness, and also see to it that you get prayer for healing. Then, you can go back to your doctor with a healthy body and testify to him of God's healing power.

Authority Power and Miracle-Working Power

To conclude, let's look at the nature of God's power to heal. If you were to read the New Testament in Greek, you would find two major words used to describe God's power. One of these words is *exousia*, and it means "authority" power. The other word is *dunamis*, which we looked at briefly in an earlier chapter, and it means "miracle-working" power; *dunamis* is "dynamite" power.

God's Word is the *exousia*, or authority, of God, and it has great power. When a person believes and appropriates the Word, it can move and change circumstances because the Word is backed by the authority of almighty God. The One who framed the universe is the most powerful authority that exists.

Every Christian has the authority of God's Word to believe for healing. Without that authority, we would have no right to expect healing.

Let me illustrate authority power. I know you have a healthy respect for that car with the revolving red and blue lights on top. Why is that? It is because the police officer behind the wheel has the authority to pull you over and make life uncomfortable if you have broken some traffic law. The officer wearing the badge doesn't have to physically drag you to traffic court. All he or she needs to do is write a ticket, and you will either have to pay the fine by mail or make a court appearance to contest the charge—at which point you will still have to pay the fine if the judge rules against you. The officer's vehicle and the badge the officer wears are symbols of the law that enforces his or her authority. God's Word is the highest law in the universe, and it is upheld by His authority power.

Now let's look at *dunamis* power. We are all familiar with what a few sticks of dynamite can do to the side of a mountain. The dynamite's explosive power will tear away tons of rock and soil. When the first atomic bomb was dropped, the entire world saw the destructive force of splitting the atom. Since then, that awesome power has held many people in nations all over the world in the grip of fear. However, it was God who created the atom. Did you know that Hebrews 1:2–3 says Jesus created the universe, and it is Jesus who holds all things *together* by the Word of His *dunamis* power? (See also Colossians 1:17.) The Lord has "dynamite" power ready to be released in miraculous ways for the benefit of all humanity.

That miracle power is more than able to save souls, transform lives, and heal physical bodies.

The greatest dimension of God's miracle-working power was unleashed at the moment when life conquered death and Jesus was raised from the dead. Jesus gives that same power to believers when they are baptized with the Holy Spirit. (See Acts 1:8.) Every time someone is born again, every time someone is healed, God's miracle-working power is demonstrated. However, miracle-working power operates only in conjunction with authority power. If we expect to experience miracles, then we must be in line with God's authority. That authority is His Word.

Jesus always exercised both *exousia* and *dunamis* power when He healed and delivered the sick and demonized. The people marveled at His ability and said, *"What a word this is! For with authority and power He commands the unclean spirits, and they come out"* (Luke 4:36). A Spirit-filled, born-again believer has been given that same ability. We have both the authority of God's Word and the miracle-working power of the Holy Spirit. Don't let the devil "do you in." Overcome him with the Word and the Spirit.

In Luke 10:19, Jesus gave believers authority power to overcome the evil powers of Satan when He said, *"Behold, I give you the authority [exousia] to trample on serpents and scorpions, and over all the power [dunamis] of the enemy, and nothing shall by any means hurt you."* Although Satan also has supernatural power, he cannot exercise that power over Christians who know how to use the Word of God against him. You are able to overcome Satan

> *Overcome Satan by the blood of the Lamb and by the word of your testimony about Jesus as Savior, Redeemer, Healer, and Deliverer.*

by the blood of the Lamb and by the word of your testimony about Jesus as Savior, Redeemer, Healer, and Deliverer. (See Revelation 12:11.) Put the Word of God in your heart and in your mouth, and Satan must bow to that authority.

I have a practical illustration of *exousia* and *dunamis*. When my children were small, we sometimes left them with a babysitter. With my word, I gave the sitter authority to care for the children while we were gone. However, if Mike or Sarah did not obey her, I had a stick. That stick was small, but it was mighty. It had amazing "dunamis" power to keep those two in line. They knew both Wally and I had the parental authority to use the dynamite of that little stick.

To the religious hypocrites of His day, Jesus said, *"You are mistaken, not knowing the Scriptures nor the power [dunamis] of God"* (Matthew 22:29). Even today, believers do not understand the necessity for the Word and the Spirit to work in agreement. Christians who are baptized with the Holy Spirit are enthusiastic about the miracle power of God. They expect to see *dunamis* at work in their lives and in others' lives, but they are often unwilling to come under the authority of God's Word in matters such as eating correctly, resting, and so forth. Their pat answer is, "I'm walking in the Spirit." These people don't believe God's rules apply to them because they think the Spirit supersedes the Word. However, the Word and the Spirit always agree! (See 1 John 5:7.)

On the other side of the coin are the fundamentalists who stand firm on the authority of God's holy Word. They claim to believe the Bible from cover to cover; they even believe the cover. These people will fight to preserve every comma and period; but when you talk to them about healing, they say, "Healing and miracles are not for today." Again, they believe that Jesus authenticated His Person and His ministry with the miraculous, but that there is no necessity for miracles today. Therefore, they rob themselves and others of God's miracle power and frustrate the grace of God. (See Galatians 2:21.) I'm convinced that no Christian would willingly sidestep the grace that was purchased for us at Calvary.

When believers don't allow the authority of the Word and the power of the Spirit to work together, they are out of balance. I want you to think of a bird. Can that bird get off the ground without two wings? Obviously not; nor can the bird sustain flight without the balance and strength of both wings. You, as a Christian, will never soar into the things of God unless you are

You will never soar into the things of God unless you are balanced with the authority of God's Word and the miraculous, supernatural power of the Holy Spirit.

balanced with the authority of God's Word and the miraculous, supernatural power of the Holy Spirit. Only with this balance can any one of us transcend the natural elements of this world and be elevated into the supernatural life of God.

I want to tell you about a woman who knew both the authority and the power of God. She exercised her faith in both areas and flew beyond the barriers of Satan and sickness into the healing, keeping power of Jesus. This lady shared her testimony in a service. Sometime previously, she had had a tumor removed from her back, but evidence of the tumor had reappeared. During the service, this lady felt the power of the Holy Spirit all over her, and she knew the tumor was gone. Moments later, the Lord showed me that someone in the audience had been healed of a tumor on the back. When I called out this healing, the woman responded. When her husband examined her back, all signs of the tumor were gone—never to return. Praise the Lord!

Christians who are not experiencing healing, or those who lose their healing, may not be living a balanced life. Some may not be accepting the reality of miracles, while others may not be coming under the authority of God's Word. First Corinthians 3:16 declares that our bodies are temples of God. However, multitudes of Christians ignore the warning in verse 17: *"If anyone defiles the temple of God, God will destroy him. For the temple of God is holy, which temple you are."* We wouldn't think of going into our church sanctuaries and defiling them in some way, such as spilling food and drink in them. However, we continually abuse our bodies with improper food and drink, lack of rest and exercise, and other bad habits that destroy the body. *"Do not be wise in your own eyes; fear the LORD and depart from evil. It will be health to your flesh, and strength to your bones"* (Proverbs 3:7–8).

We must obey God's Word and care for our bodies correctly if we are to experience healing and continue to walk in health. When you were born again, your body became God's temple, and it belongs to Him. When you abuse your body, you are hurting God and preventing Him from continually activating health in your body. Often, people excuse their bad habits by saying they just can't quit. Yes, they can. It simply takes submitting our wills to God's will as we cast all our cares upon Him. (See James 4:7; 1 Peter 5:7.) All things are possible to the one who believes. (See Mark 9:23.) Let's all be bell ringers for God!

Signs and Wonders

Everything looked hopeless; the task seemed impossible. How could it be that at the last minute the mission would be aborted? So many lives were at stake, including the lives of the men in the small boats off the coast of Siberia. However, there was not one man who hadn't known from the beginning how very dangerous this "impossible" mission was. Nevertheless, believing that God is the God of the impossible, they had undertaken the venture with hope and enthusiasm. What an opportunity had been given them to get thousands of New Testaments into the hands of the political prisoners of the Soviet Union.

The small group of men had traveled to Alaska carrying their contraband cargo of Bibles, and from Alaska they had flown to the furthermost tip of the Aleutian Islands. There, they carefully loaded the precious cargo into the small boats awaiting them, and then, under a heavy cloud cover, God's "under-cover agents" headed for the eastern coast of Siberia. These men and those who helped them had thought of everything, including sealing the New Testaments in watertight containers that would float. Now, they were at the moment upon which all depended, the moment when the Bibles would be thrown into the sea and carried ashore with the ingoing tide.

Somehow, at this crucial point, the timing had gone wrong. Instead of a rising tide, the group encountered a receding tide that would carry the Bibles out to sea instead of in to the shore. What was to be done? Every minute counted; the men's lives were at stake. If they were spotted, they would be captured. But these Christian men believed in a miracle-working God. In the name of Jesus, they commanded the tide to reverse and threw the Bibles overboard. As they slipped away unnoticed, they could see the little packages bobbing toward the shore.

Believe God for the Impossible

Unbelievable, you say? Well, it may be unbelievable to some, impossible to others, but it is true, nevertheless. This incident took place about twelve years before the collapse of the U.S.S.R., when Christians were being persecuted there and it was illegal to take Bibles into the country. We have a big God, don't we? He doesn't want us to believe Him for just the possible things in our lives. He wants us to believe Him for impossible things. It wasn't just men and women of the Bible who received miracles; men and women of faith are still receiving miracles. We serve a living Lord, and, because He lives, miracles are here to stay—they are here today!

The Bible begins with a profound yet simple statement: *"In the beginning God created the heavens and the earth"* (Genesis 1:1). This fact is the basis for everything that follows; God is the Author and Creator of all that exists. With supernatural power and genius, the Lord brought into being everything that is natural. What was so in the beginning still is to the present day; the natural is subject to the supernatural. God controls what He created. This principle is the foundation for miracles!

> *The natural is subject to the supernatural. God controls what He created. This principle is the foundation for miracles!*

And love is the reason for miracles. God created you and me, and He loves us so much that He will move mountains or *change the ocean tides* on our behalf when we link faith with His miraculous ability:

> *Now to Him who is able to do exceedingly abundantly above all that we ask or think, according to the power that works in us.*
> (Ephesians 3:20)

Miracles are not isolated within the boundaries of "Christian" nations, nor can they be prevented by hostile governments. Miracle-working faith can be found wherever the Word of God has been preached. I learned of a Russian family who was living on a farm near Chernobyl when the nuclear plant exploded. Radioactive particles contaminated the air, the water, the ground, and the people in a very large surrounding area. Since then, the world has seen the horrible results in the bodies of thousands of Russian people. The Russian government actually built a city to house and hospitalize the thousands of people who suffered from the intense radiation. Even children of affected parents have been born with horrible defects, cancers, and skin problems.

However, this particular Christian family prayed to God for a miracle. These people knew they served a God who was much bigger than a nuclear blast—a God who could protect them when everything around them was being permeated with invisible death. This family prayed and asked the Lord not only to spare them, but also to spare their livestock and their land from the contamination. The Lord answered their prayer, and they were not harmed. Later, when the government examined this family and their animals, they found them to be free of any contamination. Even the ground was clean. What had happened? The Lord who created the elements had taken control of them.

Supernatural Works by a Supernatural God

Within the pages of the Bible can be found miracles of every sort and description in which God altered the natural course of things by supernatural intervention. We read of the Red Sea opening before Israel and closing over the Egyptians, the bitter waters of Marah becoming sweet when Moses cast the tree into them, and the Jordan River rolling back when Joshua led the Israelites into the Promised Land. Elisha threw salt into the waters of Jericho and "healed" the water, which had been causing fruit trees to drop their fruit and cattle to miscarry their young. There was the borrowed ax head that Elisha recovered when it came swimming to the surface of the water after he threw a stick into the river. Jesus turned water into wine at a marriage feast. He stifled the stormy waters of Galilee, but later He and Peter walked on that same sea in the midst of a storm.

Whether Jesus stills your storm or walks you through it, He will give you victory. On my first trip to the land of Israel, the Lord took me through a terrible storm over the Atlantic. At this time, my husband, Wally, and I were leading a tour group to the Holy Land. Scarcely out of New York, the plane suddenly plummeted what seemed like thousands of feet. We were flying into a severe storm, and the plane reeled and tossed all the way across the ocean. One woman, who had mustered all her courage to take the flight, was terribly frightened. She prayed frantically for the storm to cease, but the Lord spoke these never-to-be-forgotten words into her heart: *I don't always take you out of the storm, but I will always take you through the storm.*

God not only controls the waters that He created, but He also controls all the elements. Didn't God protect the Israelites from the heat and cold of the wilderness with an enormous pillar of cloud during the day and a huge pillar of fire at night? He caused ravens to bring food to Elijah when there was a drought in the land and a meager supply of food, and those ravens did not eat any of the food intended for Elijah. The Lord kept a widow, her son, and that same prophet from starving with a continual supply of oil and meal. He saved another widow's sons from slavery by miraculously filling borrowed pots with oil. The valuable liquid was sold to pay the family's debt so that the sons would not have to be sold to pay it off.

Over and over, we see examples of the Lord miraculously supplying food for the hungry. For forty years, God fed a crowd of two million in the wilderness with manna and twice gave them water to drink out of a rock. In one instance, Elisha prayed over a pot of soup that had been accidentally poisoned by a wild herb that had been added to it. The soup was "healed," and a very hungry crowd of young prophets was able to partake of it without harm. On at least two occasions, Jesus fed a crowd of several thousand after multiplying a few loaves and fishes; but, as we just saw, God cared enough to provide a miraculous supply of food for just one starving widow.

Whatever You Need, the Lord Can Supply

God cares so much for you that there is not one sickness, not one problem, not one impossibility—humanly speaking—that He cannot turn into a miracle for you. Even if what you need does not exist, your loving heavenly Father is able to bring it into existence, whether it's a new job or a "new" body. Nothing is impossible with our God. Whatever you need, the Lord can supply, even though it may take a miracle. God is able to heal your finances as well as your body. He is able to heal your marriage and change your wayward children. Don't put your confidence in people or your present circumstances. They can change in an instant. Put your confidence in God; trust Him. The difference between those who receive their miracles and those who do not is faith. God is not a "respecter" of people (see Acts 10:34 KJV); He is a respecter of faith.

Once, a member of our congregation encountered a demonized man. During the encounter with this crazed person, the man was bitten very badly on his hand. After prayer for the wound, he washed his hurting hand and saw that all the bite marks had disappeared—and his hand was as good as new. I agree that such a thing sounds unbelievable; but if we accept only what we can believe with our natural minds, we rob ourselves of all the answers that God has for us in His realm of the supernatural. I'm for living a supernatural life where only heaven is the limit, aren't you?

Whatever fiery dart the devil flings at you—financial difficulty, illness, a broken relationship, or anything else—God is able to transform into good and use to glorify His name. The evil that destroys others need not destroy you. A fiery furnace failed to consume the three young Hebrew men who were cast into it, but it killed the soldiers who had thrown them into the fire. Hungry lions refused to eat Daniel when he was thrown into their den, but these same animals devoured the next crowd before their bodies could even fall to the floor. A great fish of the sea swallowed the drowning prophet Jonah and then vomited him onto the coast near Nineveh. The entire city repented of its wickedness when the waterlogged prophet preached in its streets; but almost two centuries later, that backslidden city was destroyed by a flood. Ironically, Nineveh was saved by water and later destroyed by water.

For the sake of Joshua, God turned defeat into victory when He stopped the sun in its heavenly course and gave His people enough daylight to defeat their enemy. We know that God turned the sundial back ten degrees as a sign of healing for Hezekiah. God cares as much for His people in this generation as He did for the people of those generations. Although we live in a day when the sun is causing skin cancer and the air we breathe is causing lung disease, the Lord will spare us from all of this when we trust Him to do it. There may be holes in the ozone above us and poisonous earth beneath us, and the water may be polluted, but our God is able to deliver us: *"A thousand may fall at your side, and ten thousand at your right hand; but it shall not come near you"* (Psalm 91:7).

God is unlimited in His authority, in His power and might, and in His mercy, compassion, and love for you. Always trust Him for the best.

Isn't the Lord able to rain gigantic hailstones on His enemies, shake the earth to open prison doors, stop the venom of poisonous snakes, deliver from demons, and rebuke sickness and death? He is not only able, but He has also done it before, and He can do it again. Don't ever limit the Lord. Believe Him to perform whatever miraculous sign or creative wonder you need. God is unlimited in His authority, unlimited in His power and might, and unlimited in His mercy, compassion, and love for you. Always trust Him for the best. When you run out of ideas, He has just begun to think of ways to deliver you!

On one of my first trips to Ethiopia, I was scheduled to fly by helicopter to a refugee camp where the starving people were anxiously waiting for help. I had gone with a large amount of food, and I wanted to get pictures of the camp to use in future endeavors to raise funds to purchase necessities for these precious people caught in the grip of famine and political revolution. When the helicopter arrived to take us to the camp, a delegation of U.S. congressmen was given precedence over me and my crew, and there was no room for us. I was not too happy, but I reminded myself that it was the Lord who had gotten me there for His purpose, and He was well able to fulfill that purpose.

So we waited, if not too patiently, for the helicopter to return for our group. When the American men returned, they were all fuming. A constant downpour of rain had prevented them from taking pictures or conducting their anticipated activity. Even though the congressmen told us our flight would be useless, we boarded the helicopter, praying and believing that the Lord hadn't brought us thousands of miles in vain. By the time we reached the refugee camp, the rain had ceased, and we were able to get all the pictures we wanted. What's more, we were able to personally begin the food distribution. You see, God had everything under control for us. My ministry partners had not wasted their money, and I had not wasted my time.

Four Components to Miraculous Living

There is no question that the Lord expects His people to be living in the supernatural, because Jesus said, *"He who believes in Me, the works that I do he will do also; and greater works than these he will do, because I go to My Father"* (John 14:12). When Jesus went to the Father, He and the Father sent back the Holy Spirit to empower believers. As a rule, the people who are seeing and experiencing the most miracles today are the Spirit-filled believers of every denomination.

Each believer should carefully examine Jesus' ministry for the keys that made Him successful and then use these keys to unlock the door to personal success as a Christian. Does that sound too much like the advice of a "success" seminar? Don't forget that Jesus walked this earth as the Son of *Man*; His resources were no more and no less divine than the resources you have as a child of God. The Holy Spirit was Jesus' source of power, and the same Holy Spirit lives and abides in you! As a man, Jesus consistently followed certain guidelines that not only produced signs and wonders but also produced a successful life and ministry. Without these things, He never would have been able to work miracles or face and endure the agony of Calvary. Here, then, are the components for living a life accompanied by signs and wonders.

1. Baptism with the Holy Spirit

We all know that when Jesus walked the earth, miraculous signs and wonders followed Him wherever He went. However, Jesus didn't begin to move in the miraculous until He was baptized with the Holy Spirit. The Lord was an unknown carpenter from Galilee, about thirty years old, when John baptized Him in the Jordan and the Father baptized Him with the Spirit. The Old Testament describes the Messiah as the *"Anointed"* (see, for example, Psalm 2:2; Isaiah 61:1–3), the One anointed with the power of God's Spirit. Not one miracle Jesus performed was done in His own strength; He walked in the power and anointing of the Holy Spirit—and so can you. (See Acts 1:8.)

2. A Commitment to Prayer

The next crucial thing that I see in Jesus' life is prayer. While the disciples slept, Jesus spent nights communing with His Father in prayer. This two-way communication was the strength of His soul, the direction finder and goal setter for all His time. Returning one noon with lunch, the disciples were astonished at their Master when they found Him already strengthened and satisfied. Jesus explained,

> *Jesus' two-way communication with the Father in prayer was the strength of His soul, the direction finder and goal setter for all His time.*

"I have food to eat of which you do not know" (John 4:32). Jesus was speaking of His prayer life. I believe that morning in prayer, the Father had instructed His Son to go through Samaria and stop at Jacob's well. If you recall, while His companions were buying lunch, Messiah introduced Himself to an adulterous woman and led her into the kingdom of God.

In John 14:14, Jesus said, *"If you ask anything in My name, I will do it."* If we are going to receive God's miraculous answers to meet our needs, then we must spend time in prayer. I think many of us miss God's best because we are not committed to a prayer life.

3. A Knowledge of, and Love for, God's Word

Jesus depended not only on the power of the Holy Spirit and time spent with His Father in prayer but also on the Word; His every attitude, purpose, and action was wholly in line with the written Word of God. Before we see miracles in Christ's life, we see Him conquer Satan by quoting the Word to him. "It is written" was the guideline for His life, and He continually spoke the Word to all those who listened to Him. The will of the Father was known to Jesus through scriptural revelation. If He had not followed the principles of the Word, He could not have fulfilled its prophecies concerning Himself.

Jesus said, *"If you love Me, keep My commandments"* (John 14:15). Our love for God is measured by our obedience to His Word. A supernatural life is reserved for those who know and love the Word.

4. *An Attitude of Thanksgiving*

A thankful heart is the next component of prime importance in Jesus' personal life and public ministry. His whole attitude was one of thanksgiving, and He set this example for everyone around Him. Jesus kept His priorities right by thanking His Father for the accomplishments of His life. He never looked to Himself; He always looked to the Father and credited Him for the work that was done. Our Lord was in the habit of thanking the Father even before He acted. Do you remember that He thanked the Father before He called Lazarus from the tomb? Gratitude marked the simple things in Jesus' life, as well as the profound. He thanked the Father before He broke bread with the disciples and before miraculously feeding the multitudes. We can have this same attitude of thanksgiving. Paul wrote, *"Rejoice in the Lord always. Again I will say, rejoice!...Be anxious for nothing, but in everything by prayer and supplication, with thanksgiving, let your requests be made known to God"* (Philippians 4:4, 6).

A Simple Lesson, Lived by Simple Faith

Let's review these four things: baptism with the Holy Spirit, prayer, God's Word, and an attitude of thanksgiving. The baptism with the Holy Spirit puts a Christian into the dimension of miracle-working power, and it enables the believer to receive and to give in a greater dimension. Next, when we put the Word into our prayers, things are going to change because the Word will not return void—it will accomplish and prosper God's will. Then, when believers get into the spirit of praise and worship out of thanksgiving to God, there is no end to the miracles that flow.

And they went forth, and preached every where, the Lord working with them, and confirming the word with signs following.
(Mark 16:20 KJV)

Keep your heart filled with thanksgiving, your mouth filled with the Word and prayer, and your eyes open to the supernatural. Miracles are not something that just "accidentally" happen; they are planned. Live according to the pattern of Jesus' life, and signs and wonders will follow you all the days of your life, just as routinely as goodness and mercy do. (See Psalm 23:6.)

This is really a very simple lesson, lived by simple faith. I say faith is simple because it is simply taking God at His Word. Faith itself is a miracle; and since you cannot produce *miracles* in your own strength, you can't produce *faith* in your own strength:

For by grace you have been saved through faith, and that not of yourselves; it is the gift of God, not of works, lest anyone should boast. (Ephesians 2:8–9)

Because faith is a gift from God, all you have to do is receive it. God has packaged the precious gift of faith within the pages of His Word: *"So then faith comes by hearing, and hearing by the word of God"* (Romans 10:17). Fill yourself with the Word, and you will be filled with faith.

I was so excited by a marvelous testimony sent to us by a retired school teacher that I must share it with you. The woman wrote that she had been diagnosed as having a tumor the size of a golf ball in the upper part of her stomach. The tumor was suspected to be cancerous and supposedly had spread throughout her body. After the lady received this report, she called our prayer line for a partner to agree with her for a miraculous healing. The two of them prayed according to Matthew 18:19, *"That if two of you agree on earth concerning anything that they ask, it will be done for them by My Father in heaven."* Together, they asked that the tumor shrink to nothing and totally disappear. From that moment, the woman continuously spoke healing Scriptures to her body and praised the Lord for her healing.

> *Fill yourself with the Word, and you will be filled with faith.*

Later, while she was sitting in the doctor's office waiting for a further examination, one of her hands became intensely hot, like coals of fire. She immediately touched the afflicted area of her body with her hand and thanked the Lord for manifesting her healing. When the specialist examined the woman, he found that the tumor had shrunk dramatically, had broken loose from the area where it had been, and was suspended in her upper intestine by a long stalk. Before the tumor could be removed, it traveled through the intestinal tract to the lower part of the colon. The specialist was able to easily pluck the pea-sized tumor from the woman's body, and he said he could take no credit for what God had miraculously done. And the woman was totally clear of any sign of cancer.

Miracles Then and Now

In Acts 3, Peter and John went to the temple at the hour of prayer, as was their custom. Remember that, at the temple gate, these two Spirit-filled men saw a beggar who had been lame from birth. When Peter caught the man's eye, he said, *"Silver and gold I do not have, but what I do have I give you: In the name of Jesus Christ of Nazareth, rise up and walk"* (verse 6). Peter took the man by the hand, and at once the man jumped to his feet and began to praise God and leap all around. Peter and John had both been baptized with the Holy Spirit; they were men of prayer who prayed according to God's Word and gave glory to God. These men who had signs and wonders in their lives were living like Jesus, just as you and I can.

Now, I want to look at another miracle in quite a different vein. The account of the sudden and miraculous deaths of Ananias and Sapphira is recorded in Acts 5:1–11. You may not view this as a good miracle, but it really is. You see, not everyone was perfect in the early church, any more than everyone is perfect in the church today. These two people lied to the Holy Spirit, and Peter said they would die for their lie. God had to deal with this sin to keep the ungodly from hurting the infant church and to show the believers the seriousness of their commitment to Christ. Peter was flowing in the Spirit, and his words were filled with power and were followed by miraculous demonstrations.

In Acts 5:12, we read that *"through the hands of the apostles many signs and wonders were done among the people."* As we have seen, verse 15 tells us that even the shadow of Peter falling on the sick and infirm apparently had the power to heal: *"So that they brought the sick out into the streets and laid them on beds and couches, that at least the shadow of Peter passing by might fall on some of them."* That account sounds as preposterous as people being healed when they received pieces of cloth taken from Paul, doesn't it? Nevertheless, believers accept what they read in the Bible. However, many discount that unusual miracles happen *today*. Let me ask, has the Holy Spirit gone on vacation?

Well, I know He went with me on a trip to China. This trip was very special because our group had taken sixteen thousand Bibles into that communist country without being detected. It was an extraordinary feat, so we were all "high" in the Spirit. However, the miracles were not over. One day, we were headed for the Great Wall when a lady in our group pointed her finger at the bus window and shouted, "In the name of Jesus, arise and walk!" Then, I saw the bent and crippled man standing in the shadow of the bus. Although the cripple neither saw nor heard the lady, he suddenly stood erect and burst out laughing. He was ecstatic over his "mysterious" healing; and, after the bus passed, we could still see him doing a little jig on the street corner. I would have to say that signs and wonders have not diminished through the ages. Didn't Jesus say we would do greater works than He?

The Holy Spirit even traveled to Russia with us on our tours. One afternoon in Kiev, the group had gone to see a beautiful old monastery. Just as we emerged from the building and stepped back onto the street, we saw two women sitting on a little bench. One of the women seemed quite feeble, and she was holding tightly to a cane. Moved with compassion, a Spirit-filled psychologist who was with us said, "In Jesus' name, get up and walk." She was close enough to cast her shadow on the two women, but the dear Russian lady had no idea that the American was speaking to her, and she certainly didn't know what she was saying. However, there are no language barriers to the Holy Spirit. The feeble little lady suddenly stood up, dropped the cane, and walked off. Her startled friend hurried up the street to catch up with her companion.

In Acts 8, the Holy Spirit led Philip the deacon to Samaria. We might think those awful Samaritans didn't deserve miracles. The Jews hated them because they were a "mongrel bunch" who were involved in idolatry and sorcery. Nevertheless, it was in this place where the Holy Spirit poured out a mighty revival that was accompanied by many amazing signs and wonders. Simon the sorcerer was saved, multitudes of other people were saved, and many were healed and delivered. When Peter and John joined Philip, they prayed, and the entire group received the baptism with the Holy Spirit. (See Acts 8:5–17.)

It is obvious that Satanism and sorcery didn't pass away with the revival in Samaria. What would have horrified people several decades ago is almost commonplace in today's society. Young people looking for meaning in their lives are being sucked into these devilish practices, and even some professional people are practicing Satanists because they have found a source of power. However, the power of God is still greater than any of Satan's power, and when these deluded individuals see the power of God at work, they willingly turn their lives over to Christ and receive His mighty power.

> *When people see the power of God at work, they willingly turn their lives over to Christ and receive His mighty power.*

I personally know two men who were Satanist priests, but now they are ministering for the Lord Jesus Christ. We are continually seeing people set free from the devil's deceptions.

In Acts 16, we find two Spirit-filled men praising and worshipping God. That doesn't sound too unusual, does it? Spirit-filled believers are always praising the Lord. However, these were unusual circumstances. These two men had just had their backs ripped open with a scourge, they had been placed in irons in the deepest dungeon of a Philippian jail, and it was midnight! What's more, they were innocent men. Even the most "turned-on" Christian might find such a situation a time to moan and groan—just a little. And yet, in the midst of their difficulties, Paul and Silas sang praises to the Lord because they *knew* their God. We looked at this account earlier in the book, focusing on how Paul's surrender to God freed him of fear. Let's look at it again now with an emphasis on God's miraculous power to bring people to faith in Him.

Paul and Silas weren't necessarily looking for a miracle, but they were open to one—and so were the gates of the prison. Suddenly, the earth shook, and those prison doors opened. It is a miracle the entire prison didn't collapse on Paul and Silas; but God knew what He was doing, and the two prisoners followed His leading. Instead of fleeing, Paul and Silas took advantage of the miraculous circumstance. The frightened jailer brought them home with him to dress their wounds, and, while they were there, the "captives" led their captor and his family to Jesus. The jailer discovered *he* was the one who was the prisoner—a prisoner of sin—but he and the members of his family were set free. (See Acts 16:16–34.)

Did you know that God can shake a home, open doors, and set prisoners free today? Here's a quote from a praise report written to our ministry: "I have been reunited with my husband after twenty-three years. We have both changed for the better; and we still love each other." The woman explained that she had finally placed the whole matter on the altar and called our prayer line to ask for the reconciliation of her entire family. She said she had no idea that her husband would return or that God could possibly straighten out their financial situation, which she described as "in a mess." Nevertheless, even as she was writing the letter, she received a call informing her of a large settlement of money that further untangled "the mess."

Let me tell you about some additional miracles. Within months, the homes of two pastors I know burned to the ground. Without a doubt, Satan intended to destroy these men, their families, and, consequently, their ministries. However, every member of each family was miraculously saved, and what Satan intended for evil has been turned to good. Both of these men have an even greater zeal for the Lord and a *fire* in their ministry. One of those homes had been older and in need of some repair, and the couple and their children who had lived there subsequently moved into a beautiful new home. Ha, ha, devil!

When Paul was miraculously converted on the road to Damascus, Satan lost one of his "best" sinners, and Jesus won a saint who evangelized a good portion of the known civilized world and wrote a large portion of the New Testament. Signs and wonders accompanied Paul wherever he went. On one occasion, Paul was stoned and dragged out of the city of Lystra. When the believers gathered around him and prayed, he stood to his feet. The next day, he walked about twenty miles to the city of Derbe. Personally, I believe that Paul was raised from the dead. But, whether he had died or not, Paul certainly received a miraculous healing. In those days, the people didn't stop stoning until a body was completely covered with a pile of boulders. Just one heavy rock would crush a skull or break a bone.

There's an almost amusing story in Acts 20:7–10. Paul was preaching to a group of people in the city of Troas, and he was very "long-winded." As a matter of fact, Paul preached until midnight, and a very tired young man named Eutychus fell asleep. Now, that wouldn't be too tragic; some people today go to sleep in church. But this fellow was sitting on the window ledge of the third-story room where the meeting was being held. Instead of tumbling to the inside, Eutychus fell three floors to the ground below—and died. Paul simply went down and raised him from the dead. Then, the happy congregation continued the meeting until daybreak.

The book of Acts is a book of signs and wonders. It is full of miracles from the first page to the last page. But did you know that Acts is the only book of the Bible that really has no ending? Why is that, you ask? The book of Acts is a record of the acts of the Holy Spirit, and He hasn't stopped acting yet in the lives of people. Time doesn't stop Him. Walls don't stop Him. Political regimes don't stop Him. "Impossible" situations don't stop Him. Incurable diseases don't stop Him. Neither does the unbelief of some people stop Him. The Holy Spirit is on the move, and I'm sure you want to move with Him. Let's all get under the spout where the glory comes out!

Once, a lady on our staff was watching a Christian television program. One of the guests on the program was a Spirit-filled Catholic priest who worked among the poor in towns on both sides of the U.S.-Mexican border. This priest reported the supernatural multiplication of food and miraculous healings, and he even told of a woman being raised from the dead after the doctor had written her death certificate. Several young, mentally disabled children who lived in a dump were completely healed. Their disability was due to protein deficiency in their diets when they were babies, and they weren't able to learn.

However, after a compassionate teacher prayed for the children, their minds became perfectly normal.

Again, people have a tendency to relegate signs and wonders to the dusty archives of biblical history or to the "big-name" evangelists. However, there are no big names in the work of the ministry. There never were, and there aren't now. The only big name is Jesus! It was in that name that Peter, Paul, James, and John prayed. Philip used that name to work miracles, and the Bible doesn't even mention the names of many who performed miracles in the only name that has miraculous power. None of these people ever considered himself to have a "big name."

The Lord took an arrogant, demanding Saul, transformed him, and renamed him Paul. As Saul, this man, who saw himself as very big and important, was an enemy of Christ and His church. Paul means "little," which is exactly how Paul saw himself after his miraculous encounter with the One whom he had persecuted. Nevertheless, Paul was able to say in the face of every circumstance, *"When I am weak, then I am strong"* (2 Corinthians 12:10). This man proved with many signs and wonders that human weakness is superimposed by the strength of Jesus when a person stays "little" enough to be hidden in Christ.

Jesus gave every believer—from the past right up to this present hour—the power of attorney to use His name. You,

> *You, too, can work the miraculous in the power of Jesus' name.*

too, can work the miraculous in the power of that name. Signs and wonders of every sort and description ought to follow you. Don't wait for some "big name" to come along; the name of Jesus has been entrusted to you.

The power in that name will heal bodies; it will heal minds; it will heal marriages; it will heal homes; it will heal finances. It will heal any circumstance. By the power vested in the name of Jesus, anything that needs healing can be healed. My challenge to you is to live in *total healing* and to take healing to others in Jesus' precious name.

About the Author

As founder and president of Marilyn Hickey Ministries, Marilyn is being used by God to help cover the earth with the Word. Her Bible teaching ministry is an international outreach via television, satellite, books, CDs, DVDs, and healing meetings. She has established an international program of Bible and food distribution, and she is committed to overseas ministry, often bringing the gospel to people who have never heard it before.

Marilyn, along with her late husband, Wallace Hickey, founded the Orchard Road Christian Center in Greenwood Village, Colorado. She has two grown children, five grandchildren, and four great-grandchildren.